Curious Folks Ask

Curious Folks Ask

162 Real Answers on Amazing Inventions, Fascinating Products, and Medical Mysteries

Sherry Seethaler

Vice President, Publisher: Tim Moore
Associate Publisher and Director of Marketing: Amy Neidlinger
Editorial Assistant: Pamela Boland
Development Editor: Kirk Jensen
Operations Manager: Gina Kanouse
Senior Marketing Manager: Julie Phifer
Publicity Manager: Laura Czaja
Assistant Marketing Manager: Megan Colvin
Cover Designer: Chuti Prasertsith
Managing Editor: Kristy Hart
Project Editor: Anne Goebel
Copy Editor: Gayle Johnson
Proofreader: Leslie Joseph
Indexer: Erika Millen
Senior Compositor: Gloria Schurick
Manufacturing Buyer: Dan Uhrig

Publishing as FT Press
Upper Saddle River, New Jersey 07458

FT Press offers excellent discounts on this book when ordered in quantity for bulk purchases or special sales. For more information, please contact U.S. Corporate and Government Sales, 1-800-382-3419, corpsales@pearsontechgroup.com. For sales outside the U.S., please contact International Sales at international@pearson.com.

Printed in the United States of America

First Printing February 2010

ISBN-10: 0-13-705738-5
ISBN-13: 978-0-13-705738-2

Pearson Education LTD.
Pearson Education Australia PTY, Limited
Pearson Education Singapore, Pte. Ltd.
Pearson Education North Asia, Ltd.
Pearson Education Canada, Ltd.
Pearson Educación de Mexico, S.A. de C.V.
Pearson Education—Japan
Pearson Education Malaysia, Pte. Ltd.

Library of Congress Cataloging-in-Publication Data:

Seethaler, Sherry, 1970-

Curious folks ask : 162 real answers on amazing inventions, fascinating products, and medical mysteries / Sherry Seethaler.

p. cm.

Includes bibliographical references and index.

ISBN 978-0-13-705738-2 (hardback : alk. paper) 1. Technology—Miscellanea. 2. Inventions—Miscellanea. 3. Chemical engineering—Miscellanea. 4. Human body—Miscellanea. 5. Diseases—Miscellanea. 6. Health—Miscellanea. 7. Consumer goods—Miscellanea. I. Title.

T47.S445 2010

600—dc22

2009047764

For everyone who has ever wondered

Contents

Acknowledgments

I am tremendously grateful for my wonderful agent, Jodie Rhodes, the vision and hard work of the FT Press Science team, and everyone responsible for the Quest section of the *San Diego Union-Tribune*, especially my three editors: Leigh Fenly, Margaret King, and Scott LaFee. Of course, *Curious Folks Ask* would not have been possible without the curious folks who asked the questions that have taught me so much over the years. No matter how quickly the days pass, or how busy they seem to be, may we all find time each day to wonder.

About the Author

Sherry Seethaler is a science writer and educator at the University of California, San Diego. She works with scientists to communicate their discoveries to the public. She also writes a weekly column for the *San Diego Union-Tribune* in which she answers readers' questions spanning nearly every imaginable science topic. She earned a Bachelor of Science in biochemistry and chemistry from the University of Toronto, a Master of Science and a Master of Philosophy in biology from Yale University, and a Doctor of Philosophy in science and mathematics education from the University of California, Berkeley. She is also the author of *Lies, Damned Lies, and Science* (FT Press Science, 2009). It serves as a guide and set of tools for making sense of the health and science-related issues we encounter in our daily lives.

Preface

Inquiring minds want to know. What's the big deal about low-carb diets? What causes muscle aches when you get the flu? How did the ancient Egyptians build the Giza Pyramids? Does it matter what brand of gasoline you buy? Could adult stem cells have as much promise as embryonic stem cells? Is a horsepower really the power of one horse? Does chocolate cause acne? What makes glue sticky? How is it possible to design bifocal contact lenses? What causes dandruff?

And sometimes, inquiring minds ask questions that other inquiring minds did not even realize they wanted to know. Why do we get skin cancer from sun-damaged skin when damaged cells are continually sloughing off and being replaced? What causes out-of-body experiences? Is the *Star Wars* lightsaber possible? Are there beneficial viruses, just as there are beneficial bacteria? Why do some people have second toes that are longer than their big toes? Is increased environmental noise leading to increased violence? With their unwieldy number system, how did the ancient Romans engineer their magnificent buildings?

These are some of the 162 questions compiled in this science Q&A anthology. The questions come from real people who range in age from high schoolers to octogenarians (and probably even younger and older folks too). Some of them are scientists, and others tell me, "I'm not a science person, but I've always wanted to know..." What they share is a deep curiosity about the world around them. The questions and answers in *Curious Folks Ask* can rekindle the natural wonder about science and the world around us that we all shared as children but that frequently gets pushed aside in formal education settings.

Since I began writing a weekly science Q&A for the *San Diego Union-Tribune* in 2004, not a week has gone by that I haven't learned something surprising from answering readers' questions. People often ask me if I know the answers off the top of my head. Sometimes I do, or think I do, but I extensively research each answer because, after all, science is constantly progressing. There is always something new—perhaps a different way of thinking about things, a controversy where none was evident initially, or a myth that has masqueraded as the truth for so long that many well-informed people have been fooled.

For example, the notion that getting chilled can cause one to catch a cold is dismissed as an old wives' tale by many usually reliable sources. However, a careful search of the peer-reviewed scientific literature turns up a more interesting story, which is revealed in the first Q&A in Chapter 5. This illustrates a unique feature of *Curious Folks Ask*. The concise, palatable answers highlight not just what is known, but also where gaps in scientific understanding exist. Perhaps these mysteries will even inspire a young reader or two to take up the torch and begin a journey into scientific research.

This book is organized into eight chapters of questions and answers about humans and our creations, encompassing a plethora of topics in human biology, rounded out with a touch of chemistry and physics. Individual Q&As are self-contained but are grouped according to the natural themes that arise in people's questions. The questions range from the products of our civilization, to our bodies and how they work, to the nemeses that bring us down, to what makes us tick, to the latest health fads.

- Chapter 1, "Ingenious Inventions." Whether high-tech or seemingly mundane, ancient or futuristic, interesting science is behind every one of our inventions. Folks ponder their origins, how they work, and how to troubleshoot them.
- Chapter 2, "Chemical Concoctions." Chemical-free is the latest silly buzzword being used to market food, personal-care products, and other stuff. Of course, everything, including us, is made of chemicals. Questions about fuel, soap, decaffeination, glue, and more provide insights into the amazing power of chemistry to transform our lives.
- Chapter 3, "Body Parts." Wisdom teeth, appendix, knuckles, and toes—our body parts are mysterious, and sometimes downright odd. How we get our parts, why we have them, and what they do are some of the things people ponder.
- Chapter 4, "Bodily Functions." Itching, yawning, sneezing, sweating—our bodies are rather busy, even when we are doing nothing. Kids, and folks who have grown into perfectly civilized adults, wonder how and why their bodies work as they do.
- Chapter 5, "Pesky Pathogens." Viruses, bacteria, and now prions sure do make it hard to stay healthy. No matter how far medicine advances, they continue to outsmart us. How to keep ahead of

these pesky, and sometimes deadly, pathogens is never far from people's minds.

- Chapter 6, "Assorted Ailments." When we are not under siege by microbes, we still have aches and pains, illnesses, and embarrassing conditions. Young and old alike ask what causes them and why they occur.
- Chapter 7, "Uniquely Human." How we got here, what sets us apart from our fellow creatures, and what makes us feel a certain way may be age-old questions, but modern research is constantly providing a fresh perspective.
- Chapter 8, "Health Nuts." Health advice seems to change every time we pick up a newspaper. From carbs, to free radicals, to gaining the most benefit from exercise, health nuts want the real scoop.

It's all here: the myths, mysteries, oddities, familiar but strange, everyday to exotic. Each answer succinctly synthesizes the current state of a body of research so that you can answer the "whys" of a child in your life, captivate people at cocktail parties, or just satisfy your own inquiring mind.

1

Ingenious inventions

Iceless icebox

How does a frost-free freezer work?

In a non-frost-free freezer, water vapor from the air condenses and then freezes on the cooling coils in the freezer (or on the plastic of the freezer compartment covering the coils). If you put off defrosting long enough, eventually so much ice accumulates that there is no longer room for even a TV dinner.

Frost-free freezers prevent this buildup by doing a mini-defrost every six hours or so. A timer turns on a heating coil, which surrounds the cooling coils, and a temperature sensor turns off the heater when the temperature starts rising above freezing.

Full of cold air

How does canned air work? Why is the air cold when it comes out of the can?

The air or gas in the can is under pressure, and it expands as it escapes from the can. Inside the can, where the gas molecules are closer together, there are attractive forces (albeit weak) between the molecules.

Because of these forces, heat energy is needed to separate the molecules. The heat comes from the environment or your skin if it is near the nozzle where the gas escapes.

Most refrigerators and air conditioners work by taking advantage of the cooling effect of an expanding gas (or a liquid expanding into a gas). Refrigerator coils contain a gas that the compressor squeezes into a liquid. Compressing the gas generates heat, which escapes through the coils on the back of the refrigerator.

An expansion valve is then opened between the compressed liquid and the heat-exchange coils inside the refrigerator. The abrupt drop in pressure, akin to releasing the nozzle on canned air, causes the liquid to expand rapidly into a gas. As the expansion occurs, heat from the inside of the refrigerator is transferred to the gas.

Air conditioners are similar to refrigerators, except that air conditioners also have fans to help move the cool air into the inside and dissipate the warm air outside.

May the Force be with you

Is a lightsaber (yes, the Star Wars sword) possible?

Glow-in-the-dark Halloween costume accessories aside, it is not possible to solidify light or make it terminate in midair. However, in his book *Physics of the Impossible*, physicist Michio Kaku explains how to make something akin to a lightsaber. Plasma—an extremely hot ionized gas—could be confined to a hollow rod dotted with small holes that would allow the glowing plasma to escape. Plasma can be hot enough to cut steel. The plasma saber would have to be plugged into a high-energy power supply, though, so it would be more unwieldy than the George Lucas version.

Sci-fi science

A popular weapon in science fiction is a "graser," or gamma-ray laser. Has anyone built one? Does any theory suggest that it is or is not possible? What would be likely uses?

Gamma-ray lasers are technically possible. Lasers that produce emissions in the microwave, infrared, visible, ultraviolet, and even X-ray ranges already exist. The trick to producing gamma rays is finding an adequate lasing medium. This is a substance (gas, liquid, or solid) that gets excited when energy is pumped in. It releases that energy as photons, or particles of light, when it returns to the unexcited state.

In other types of lasers, it is the electrons within the atoms of the lasing medium that get excited to higher energy levels. Whether the photons released are lower-energy microwaves or higher-energy X-rays depends on the size of the energy gap between the electrons' excited and relaxed states.

Gamma rays are too energetic to be produced by electrons jumping from a high to low energy level. Instead, they are produced when an atom's nucleus switches from a high to low energy state. In laser light, photon emission is organized, but getting gamma-ray photons to move in step with each other requires many nuclei to change energy states in unison. This is trickier than getting electrons to change states in unison.

A few elements, including hafnium, have an excited nucleus state that is long-lived, so these elements show promise as a lasing medium for a gamma-ray laser. The U.S. Department of Defense is interested in the problem because a gamma-ray laser would be a formidable weapon.

The laser would also have many nonmilitary applications. For instance, it could be used to probe atoms and molecules to gain an unprecedented understanding of their structure and function, to treat cancerous tumors, or to kick-start nuclear fusion for energy production.

Catching a wave

Why does my radio crackle with static or some other interference? This occurs on AM stations—in particular, more loudly on distant stations and not as badly on some local stations. Is there any way to eliminate this problem?

Many natural sources (static electricity, lightning, solar flares) and man-made sources (motors, electrical equipment) can interfere with radio reception. AM is more susceptible to static than FM because of differences in the characteristics of the transmitted radio signal.

In AM—amplitude modulation—the height of the radio waves, if you visualize them as waves on the ocean, varies according to the signal. In FM—frequency modulation—it is not the height of the waves, but rather the number of waves passing a given point each second, that encodes your favorite music or radio show. Most interference affects the amplitude rather than the frequency of a radio signal.

In addition, radio waves in the frequency range transmitted by AM radio (near 1 megahertz), but not FM (near 100 megahertz), can reflect off the ionosphere, the upper layer of the atmosphere. Since radio waves travel in straight lines, the curvature of the Earth limits their range. Bouncing off the ionosphere and being reflected to Earth allows AM radio waves to travel long distances compared to (ground-based) FM signals. However, interactions with the ionosphere create static, so more distant AM stations have more static than local ones.

You cannot eliminate natural sources of static, but here are some tips for improving radio reception. Turn off any unneeded appliances. Touch lamps or lamps with dimmer switches may need to be unplugged. If practical, try moving your radio to different places in the house (for example, a windowsill) to see where reception is best.

Just turning the radio or moving the power cord can help, because sometimes the AM radio antenna is inside the radio, and sometimes it is in the cord. It is also possible to purchase an external AM loop antenna for some radios. In the case of your car radio, examine the base of the antenna for signs of corrosion.

Out, damned spot!

After I wash my car windows and let them air-dry on a bright, sunny day, I notice a grid of circles about the size of quarters visible on the glass that wasn't there before I washed them. On other cars, the grid is sometimes slightly differently sized and sometimes not perfect circles.

These are mineral deposits, such as calcium and iron, left behind when water evaporates. The pattern depends on how the water evaporates (how well water sheets from your car, the amount of wind, and so on). Also, the concentration of minerals varies in water from different sources.

Vinegar, a weak acid, can help dissolve the minerals and is supposedly the secret of expert car detailers. However, it will remove any wax on your car and cannot fix the paint if the minerals have etched it. Auto aficionados seeking to prevent mineral deposits can purchase a water deionizer that attaches to a garden hose.

Glass stretch marks

I have seen a grid of circles on the factory-provided window tints that also appear to act as the laminate layer. This is especially true on the rear windows of older BMWs after you wash them. It can be seen more prominently with polarized sunglasses. It still looks like a pattern of regular circles about the size of quarters throughout the entire glass.

If (as just discussed) the circles are due to mineral deposits left behind as water evaporates, they should appear on all the windows as well as the paint. Also, they will not form a perfectly regular grid.

On the other hand, if the pattern is very regular, and you see it on only the rear and side windows, the grid is part of the safety glass itself. The rear and side windows are usually made from tempered glass, and the tempering process creates a stress pattern that is visible within the glass.

To temper glass, it is heated to 1,200 degrees F (650 degrees C), and then the outer surface of the glass is cooled rapidly by blowing air over it. The center of the glass cools more gradually. As it cools, it contracts, compressing the outer surfaces of the glass together and creating a stress pattern along the midplane of the glass.

Tempered glass is stronger than regular glass, but when it does break, the internal stress causes the glass to shatter into many small pieces. Since it would be dangerous if a stone shattered the windshield while someone was driving, the windshield is made from laminated safety glass. Some upscale auto manufacturers offer laminated safety glass in side windows for added occupant safety and break-in resistance.

Laminated safety glass consists of two sheets of nontempered glass sandwiched together with a sheet of vinyl in the middle, to which the glass adheres when it breaks. Windows made from laminated safety glass lack the grid of circles characteristic of windows made from tempered glass.

The rear windows of certain cars with window tints definitely have a more noticeable grid pattern. It is possible that the plastic tinted layer has some pattern associated with it, but it is more likely that the tint acts like polarized sunglasses to block some of the scattered light, making it easier to discern the stress pattern in the tempered glass.

Seeing double

Since contact lenses move with your eyes as they move, how are bifocal contact lenses possible?

One bifocal contact lens design—called alternating, or translating, vision—is similar to bifocal glasses. Each lens has two segments. The distance correction is on top, and the near correction is below. The eye moves between the two lens powers as the gaze shifts up and down.

Conversely, simultaneous-vision lenses are designed so that the eyes look through both near and distance powers at once, and the visual system determines which power to use.

Alternating-bifocal contact lenses can be weighted, or slightly flattened at the base, so that the lens is supported by the lower lid and is shifted upward relative to the pupil when the gaze is directed downward.

The simplest form of simultaneous vision is monovision. One eye, usually the dominant one, is fitted with the distance correction, and the other eye is fitted with the near correction. More complicated designs are concentric ring lenses and aspheric lenses. Concentric ring designs feature a bull's-eye pattern of the near and far prescriptions. Aspheric designs have the two powers blended across the lens.

Because simultaneous-vision lenses maintain both the near and far prescription powers in front of the pupil at all times, both powers focus light onto the retina. Therefore, the retina receives two images—one that is in focus and one that is out of focus. Over time, the brain learns to make sense of this strange state of affairs by paying attention to the clear image and ignoring the superimposed out-of-focus image.

The adaptation is not perfect. Monovision reduces depth perception because only one eye receives a clear image of any scene. Simultaneous lenses with more than one power per lens reduce visual acuity—the sharpness of an image—because the out-of-focus image creates a veiling effect on the retina.

Another problem with bifocal contact lenses is that the way lenses fit over an individual's cornea is unique. As a result, it is not easy to predict where the optical center of the lens will be and whether the power zones will line up correctly with the pupil.

Because of these challenges, bifocal contact lenses are not as popular as single-prescription lenses. However, the technology has improved, and there are more designs to choose from. Which design is best for an individual depends on the shape of the eye as well as a person's lifestyle and activities.

Say what?

Why is it so difficult to make a hearing aid that works?

Designing a good hearing aid is actually a difficult engineering problem. When people suffer hearing loss, they often lose the ability to hear some sounds but not others. For example, presbycusis—age-related hearing loss—usually first diminishes the ability to hear higher-pitched sounds.

Therefore, if a hearing aid simply amplified all sounds equally, the sounds that were already audible would become uncomfortably loud. For this reason, hearing aids need to be adjusted to each patient's particular hearing deficits.

Hearing aids also must amplify speech sounds while minimizing background noise. Directional microphones can help, because a listener usually turns to face a person who is speaking, allowing the microphone to pick up the voice but not sounds from other directions. However, random noise can come from the same direction as the speaker's voice, especially if sounds reverberate substantially off surfaces in the room.

Sometimes the solution to one problem leads to another. For example, reducing the size of hearing aids is desirable, not just for comfort and aesthetics, but also to minimize the occlusion effect—that hollow sound of one's own voice when something blocks the ear canals. Unfortunately, shrinking the device places the microphone closer to the hearing aid output and increases feedback. Feedback occurs when some of the amplified sound is fed back to the microphone in a repeating cycle, causing an annoying whistle or squeal.

The technology is improving gradually; the hearing aid industry has been transitioning from analog to digital devices. Digital permits more sophisticated sound processing to enhance speech and reduce feedback and background noise.

On the road again

Assuming all things are equal, does a car get better mileage if the road is wet or dry, the air is very humid or dry, the altitude is high or at sea level, the temperature is very cold or very hot?

According to members of SAE International (the Society of Automotive Engineers), a car gets better mileage:

- When the road is dry. This is because the tires get better traction, and the power is transferred to the road more efficiently.
- In humid conditions. This is because there is less need to throttle the engine. Throttling is a way of controlling the speed of an internal combustion engine, but it consumes some of the engine's power.

  An internal combustion engine is a cylinder in which air and gasoline are mixed, compressed by a piston, and ignited. In the first step of the four-stroke combustion cycle used by most cars, a valve opens to take in air and gasoline as the piston moves downward. Throttling closes the intake valve for part of the time the piston is moving downward, forcing the piston to pull against a partial vacuum, which wastes energy.

  For a particular power output, the engine needs a constant amount of oxygen to burn the required amount of fuel. When more water molecules are in the air, some of the oxygen molecules are displaced. Therefore, in humid conditions, the engine must take in a greater volume of air to get the same amount of oxygen. The intake valve can remain open longer, and less work is required to pump the gases through the engine.
- At high altitude. This is because there is less drag on a vehicle in thinner air. It also takes less effort to expel the exhaust, because the atmospheric pressure "pushing back" on the engine is lower. In addition, less throttling occurs, because a larger volume of air must be taken in to get enough oxygen to burn the same amount of fuel.
- When it is very hot (assuming the air conditioning is off). This is because the air density is lower, so, for the same reason just described, there is less need to throttle the engine.

You may not be able to change where you drive or the weather conditions, but making certain that your tires are properly inflated is an excellent way to improve mileage. Inflating them to more than the manufacturer's recommendation can reduce traction, but inflating too little can reduce the size of your wallet. With too little air, the tires flatten out, resulting in increased rolling friction, which slows down the wheel and decreases gas mileage.

Kooky clocks

As I was engaged in my weekly chore of raising the weights and slightly resetting the time on our 1780s grandfather clock, I wondered how people of that era could accurately set their clocks, which undoubtedly gained or lost at least a minute or two every week. I assume that those with almanacs could try to approximate the time by coordinating with sunrise or sunset, but I don't know if that's true. So how did they set their clocks?

In the late 1700s, the almanac, with its elaborate tables of astronomical and seasonal events, was important in keeping track of time. But back then people still relied on the rising and setting of the sun to mark time. They were much less obsessed than we are now with accurate timekeeping.

In fact, until the late 1800s, cities and towns had independent times, depending on their observation of the sun. Time zones were not considered necessary until trains crisscrossed the country. Pressure from the railroads led the U.S. government to divide the country into four time zones, which were synchronized at noon on November 18, 1883 when the master clock at the U.S. Naval Observatory transmitted the time to major cities via telegraph.

Lost with digital

Why is it possible to point your watch's hour hand toward the sun and then find south between the hour hand and the 12 (assuming you're in the Northern Hemisphere)? How does this relate to sundials?

The sun reaches its high point in the sky at astronomical noon—a moment also known as the meridian. (It comes from the same Latin stem as the terms *ante meridiem*, or a.m., and *post meridiem*, or p.m.) In the Northern Hemisphere, the sun is due south at the meridian because only between the Tropic of Cancer and the Tropic of Capricorn is the sun ever directly overhead.

Therefore, at noon, the shadow cast by a sundial's shadow maker—the gnomon—points directly north. For a sundial to tell time, the noon mark must be oriented to true (celestial, not magnetic) north.

As the Earth rotates, the sun appears to move from east to west around the sky, and the shadow cast by the gnomon moves clockwise 15 degrees per hour (360 degrees in 24 hours).

Think of your watch as a little sundial. If you line up the hour hand with a shadow cast by the sun, you can look to the 12 to find the north/south line. However, because 360 degrees on a watch corresponds to 12 hours rather than 24, the north/south line runs through a point halfway between the hour and the 12. This point faces north between 6 a.m. and 6 p.m., after which it faces south.

Even correcting for daylight saving time, your watch is not a perfect measure of direction, because it is set according to your time zone, but astronomical noon varies across a time zone. Also, because of the Earth's tilt on its axis and its elliptical orbit around the sun, successive astronomical noons are sometimes more and sometimes less than 24 hours apart, causing up to an additional quarter hour difference between watch and sun time.

Era arrangement

The date designations B.C. and A.D. (before Christ and after the death of Christ) seem to leave a gap. In other words, how do we account for the time of Christ's life between these designations? It looks like there is a 30-year life span or so that cannot be included in either the designation "before his life" or "after his death."

A.D. is from Latin, meaning *anno Domini* or "in the year of our Lord." The monk Dionysius Exiguus, who worked out the B.C./A.D. system in the sixth century, assigned A.D. 1 to the year he thought Christ was born. However, most religious scholars place the birth of Christ between 4 and 7 B.C. by comparing what is said in the Bible to known historical and astronomical events.

Let there be light

In 2007, Congress changed the dates on which daylight saving time begins and ends. Have any studies been done to determine if DST has overall economic or societal benefits? I believe it was invented by Benjamin Franklin to aid farmers, but we are far from an agrarian society today.

Benjamin Franklin is often credited with proposing daylight saving time in the *Journal de Paris* in 1784, but his essay was a tongue-in-cheek recommendation that people go to bed earlier and get up earlier. (See http://webexhibits.org/daylightsaving/franklin3.html.)

DST was not adopted until World War I. The rationale was to conserve energy by aligning traditional work hours with daylight hours to reduce the need for artificial light. Farmers, who disliked having to deliver their goods earlier in the day, successfully fought to get DST repealed after WWI. DST was not readopted until WWII.

Between 1945 and 1966, localities could choose when to observe DST. Mass confusion resulted, with radio and TV stations and transportation companies needing to publish new schedules every time a locality began or ended DST. The Uniform Time Act of 1966 addressed this problem by stipulating that any state that chose to observe DST had to begin on the last Sunday of April and end on the last Sunday of October.

Some studies suggest that DST reduces traffic accidents because the evening rush hour occurs during daylight. On the other hand, one study showed that more accidents occur the Monday after we spring forward, probably because commuters are sleep-deprived and/or in a rush.

Proponents of DST cite figures from a 1975 U.S. Department of Transportation study conducted when DST was extended during the oil embargo. The study found that DST reduced the national electricity load by about 1 percent. In 2001, the California Energy Commission estimated that daily electricity consumption would drop by about 0.5 percent if DST were extended through the winter months.

Energy consumption is thought to decrease during DST because people use less electric lighting in the evenings, which is only partly offset by an increase in the use of lights in the morning. People are also drawn outdoors when there is sunlight and therefore use household appliances less frequently.

However, some studies that examined system-wide energy use, including commercial and residential lighting, as well as heating and air conditioning, found no effect or even negative effects of DST, depending on the climate. Also, some studies suggest an overall energy penalty, considering how much the electricity conservation is offset by people taking advantage of the daylight by using more gasoline to go places in the evenings.

Since 2007, DST runs from the second Sunday in March to the first Sunday in November. Because commerce and lifestyles have changed dramatically since many of the studies on the energy-saving potential of DST were conducted, Congress will review the impact of the DST change and reserves the right to revoke it.

Temperature tales

Can you give me a clear and reasonable explanation of the basis of the Fahrenheit scale? We all know that the Celsius or Centigrade scale is based on the freezing and boiling points of water at sea level, but so far nobody has been able to tell me how the Fahrenheit scale was created.

Most historians agree that Daniel Fahrenheit modified a scale developed by the Danish astronomer Ole Rømer. Rømer's scale had fewer subdivisions and placed the freezing point of water at a fractional degree, which Fahrenheit found cumbersome. There are conflicting accounts about how Fahrenheit calibrated his thermometers, but in a paper he wrote in 1724, Fahrenheit described using three fixed points (as translated in *A History of the Thermometer and Its Use in Meteorology*, by W. E. Knowles Middleton, 1966).

To get the 0 on his scale, Fahrenheit said he used a mixture of ice, salt, and water. For his second calibration point, at 32 degrees, he used a mixture of ice and water.

Fahrenheit wrote that the third point was fixed at 96 degrees, where "the spirit expands" when the thermometer is held under the armpit or in the mouth of a healthy person long enough to acquire the heat of the body. (Later Fahrenheit's model thermometers were recalibrated, and normal body temperature ended up at 98.6 degrees.)

Although these are Fahrenheit's words, Middleton points out that they may not be completely accurate because, as an instrument maker, Fahrenheit might have wanted to conceal his methods.

Spying on Martians

Why don't we use the Hubble telescope to look at Mars? If it can take such great pictures from deep space, it seems pictures of Mars should be possible. Can the Hubble view something this close?

The Hubble Space Telescope is useful for studying objects in the solar system (other than the Earth, which is too close). Only space probes that have passed close to Mars have been able to take clearer pictures of the planet than Hubble. Hubble has been used to monitor the atmosphere of Mars to better understand its weather patterns, particularly to gain insight into what causes the enormous dust storms that occur periodically.

Otherworldly

To what extent has data from the Hipparcos astrometric satellite been used to identify stars with planets, and to what extent could this data be used if fully exploited for this purpose? Why hasn't Hipparcos led to identification of thousands of stars with planets?

Hipparcos (HIgh-Precision PARallax COllecting Satellite) was the first space mission dedicated to measuring the distances, motions, colors, and brightness of stars. The mission was named in honor of the second-century B.C. Greek astronomer who, without a telescope, developed a catalog of 1,080 stars.

The distance to a star can be determined mathematically from its apparent shift in position, or parallax, as compared six months apart, when the Earth has revolved from one side of the sun to the other. The Hipparcos satellite was able to determine the distance to more than a million stars with unprecedented accuracy because the satellite was unobstructed by the Earth's atmosphere, which blurs the starlight reaching telescopes on Earth.

Searching for planets was not one of the goals of the Hipparcos mission. It fact, it was during the time period that Hipparcos was collecting data (1989 to 1993) that the first planets outside the solar system were detected, and the search for extrasolar planets was becoming a hot area in astronomy.

Hipparcos took multiple measurements of the same stars over time. It could detect the dimming of starlight caused by the shadow of a planet passing in front of a star.

Hipparcos detected the dimming of the star 51 Pegasi in 1991, but no one noticed until astronomers monitoring the star from the ground observed the phenomenon in 1999. This prompted the Hipparcos astronomers to reexamine the data from the mission.

Astronomers estimate that only about 10 percent of planets would pass directly in front of a star as seen from a particular vantage point. Also, it is difficult to detect the reflected light from planets directly, because the light from the star drowns it out. Therefore, most planets are detected indirectly from the "wobble" of a star caused by the planet's gravitational pull. Hipparcos was not designed to detect wobble.

Still, Hipparcos measurements are playing an important role in the search for planets. Hipparcos data on the distance to the stars is helping astronomers determine the mass of the objects causing the wobble. Mass is important because it reveals whether a star's wobble is due to the presence of a planet or another star (which would be much more massive than a planet).

Hundreds of planets have been detected outside our solar system. See http://planetquest.jpl.nasa.gov/ for the latest count.

Earthling outpost

We continue to learn a lot about the universe with the Hubble Telescope, but what are we learning with the International Space Station?

The International Space Station research program was envisioned to be highly diverse and multidisciplinary and to include both basic and applied science. However, NASA's plans for the use of the space station narrowed after President Bush's Vision for Space Exploration was announced in 2004. Fundamental research in life sciences and microgravity continues, but a major emphasis is preparing for long-duration space missions.

Data is being collected on the effects of space flight and microgravity on human health. Previously, bodily processes such as fluctuations in levels of vitamins, minerals, and hormones could be measured only before and after space flight. Now, the time course of physiological changes can be studied because of the addition of a minus-80-degree freezer on the space station. The freezer is used to store the biological samples collected during the mission until they can be returned to Earth for analysis.

One significant problem for astronauts living in a microgravity environment is loss of bone mineral density. Bone mineral density declines at an average rate of about 1 percent per month on the space station, more than 10 times faster than the average loss in postmenopausal women.

In one study, astronauts wore sensors to measure the forces on legs and feet during daily activities on the space station. The results are being used to design better exercise programs and equipment to curb bone loss in astronauts on future expeditions.

The performance and degradation of hundreds of materials are also being tested in a series of experiments mounted outside the space station. The space environment exposes materials to atomic oxygen, cycles of heating and cooling, radiation, and collisions with small meteoroids. Materials that perform well will be considered for use on satellites and future space exploration vehicles.

Crystallization, melting, solidification, and the behavior of fluids are also being studied. Since these processes are different in zero-gravity conditions, the results of the experiments will address unanswered questions in physics and help in designing better ways to manufacture various materials.

The astronauts on the space station have a great view of Earth, and they have collected hundreds of thousands of images. They observe glaciers and floating rafts of ice, wispy clouds in the upper atmosphere, brilliantly colored auroras, and sprites—flashes of light occurring in the upper atmosphere over thunderstorms. They have also captured unique, high-spatial-resolution shots of city lights and are studying the ecological effects of industrial activities. These observations will reveal long-term planetary changes.

Man or machine

The data you speak of about what we are learning from International Space Station research was quite adequately collected by the Russians during* Mir's *11 years in orbit. There is no valid mission for the International Space Station. I suggest you research the use of humans versus robots for space exploration.

Many unanswered questions about the effects of spaceflight on human health, as well as fundamental questions in materials science, can be explored in the microgravity environment on the International Space Station. However, my description of the space station research was not intended to make the case for a human space program. Whether there is an interesting research plan for the space station is a different question than whether that research justifies the cost of building and maintaining it. The latter is not a purely scientific question.

The total cost to complete the International Space Station is projected to be well over $100 billion, shared by the United States, Russia, Japan, Canada, and several European countries. NASA spends about $2 billion per year on the space station. In addition, it spends approximately $4 billion on the Space Shuttle, which is mainly used to service the space station.

The rationale offered by proponents of manned spaceflight is the human need to explore and the power of manned spaceflight to excite the public. Proponents of human spaceflight acknowledge that geopolitics has always been a large driving force behind government spending on the space program, but they argue that science ultimately benefits. They say it is important to put things into context: NASA's budget is a tiny percentage of the size of the U.S. defense budget.

The main scientific argument in favor of manned space exploration is that humans can make critical decisions about data collection. For example, although three unmanned Soviet probes collected and returned rock samples from the moon, the Apollo astronauts identified and collected samples that were considerably more diverse and consisted of 1,000 times as much material.

Critics of manned space exploration say that the expense and risk to human life outweigh the benefits. They do not dispute that manned spaceflights have yielded important scientific knowledge, but they argue that robotic missions are revolutionizing our knowledge of the solar system and are becoming even more effective and efficient as the technology improves.

For example, scientists are still learning about Saturn and its moon Titan from the data provided by Cassini and the Huygens probe, and about Mars from the rovers Spirit and Opportunity. The Cassini/Huygens and Spirit/Opportunity missions cost $3 billion and $1 billion, respectively.

Play ball

When shooting free throws, some basketball players have a very low arc, and others have a high one. Some players like to shoot off the backboard. Has it ever been proven which strategies are best from a mathematical or scientific viewpoint? Also, in baseball, coming off the bat, what angle of the ball gives the most distance?

In basketball, using the backboard provides about a 50 percent better chance of succeeding for close shots (except for very tall players, who can dunk), according to the paper "Basketball Shooting Strategies," published in *Sports Engineering*.

Energy absorbed as the ball bounces off the backboard helps compensate for shooting error. As a player gets farther from the basket, the advantage of the backboard diminishes.

The merits of the overhand push shot compared with the underhand loop shot are still disputed. Underhand shots are more stable and allow a player to put more spin on the ball. Overhand shots decrease the distance to the hoop and minimize the velocity of release.

The optimal angle of release for the basketball depends on a player's position. For instance, in "Basketball Shooting Strategies" it was determined to be 48 degrees (upward from horizontal) for a player attempting a 3-point jump shot 20 feet from the basket, releasing the ball 8 feet above the floor.

In baseball, mathematical models to determine the optimal batting angle must take into consideration nearly 30 factors. These include the physical features of the ball and bat, and the spin, speed, and direction of the pitched ball.

The optimal bat swing angle decreases from about 9 degrees (upward from horizontal) to 7 degrees as the pitch changes from fastball with backspin, to knuckleball with no spin, to curveball with topspin, according to the paper "How to Hit Home Runs," published in the *American Journal of Physics*.

Undercutting the ball center with the bat also helps maximize the ball's range. Optimal undercut is about an inch. Slightly less undercut is needed for a curveball than for a fastball.

Undercutting gives the ball backspin. Because of an aerodynamic lift force, a baseball projected with backspin travels farther than one without. However, a baseball can be projected faster without spin. Therefore, optimal batting trades off spin and speed.

Slow curveballs pitched with topspin can be batted farther than fastballs with backspin because a ball with initial topspin has a larger outgoing backspin. But for a given pitch type, batting range increases with pitch speed.

Pharaoh's secrets

What is the most widely accepted method by which the Egyptians built the Giza Pyramids?

Most Egyptologists believe that the pyramid is the natural evolution of the burial system, which began with a simple pit and progressed to the mastaba—a rectangular structure made of brick or stone. The first known Egyptian pyramid, the Step Pyramid of Djoser, probably began as a mastaba and was expanded by adding successively smaller mastabas on top.

In the century between the construction of the Step Pyramid and the Great Pyramid at Giza, the ancient Egyptians perfected their craft through trial and error. For example, some archaeologists believe that the tower-like Meidum Pyramid began as a step pyramid and suffered a catastrophic collapse during an attempt to convert it into a true pyramid.

The collapse at Meidum may have occurred while the Bent Pyramid was being constructed. If so, this could explain why the angle of ascent decreases abruptly partway up the Bent Pyramid, and why the construction technique also changed at this bend. Up to the bend, the stones in the pyramid body were laid to slope inward. After the bend, and in later pyramids, the stones were laid horizontally, a more stable configuration.

Construction on the Great Pyramid of Giza began about 2600 B.C. It is estimated to have taken 20 years and perhaps 30,000 workers (although estimates vary widely). The builders were likely a combination of skilled craftsmen and peasants who were unable to farm during the Nile's flood season.

Some of the stone was quarried nearby, and some came from upriver and was transported by barge at flood time. It is thought that the ancient Egyptians possessed no tools more sophisticated than levers, rollers, and bronze saws. Sleds lubricated with water may have been used to drag the stones up a ramp to the growing pyramid. As each new layer of stone was laid, the ramp was extended in length, as well as height, to keep its slope constant.

The workmanship of the Great Pyramid is extraordinary. For example, it rests on a base of limestone blocks that is within half an inch of being perfectly level. Such accuracy was likely achieved by flooding the area, leaving just the high spots exposed. These would be cut down, some water released, and the process repeated until the base was level.

The Great Pyramid still holds many mysteries. One is the purpose of the four "air shafts" that run diagonally through it. Such shafts would have been a construction nightmare and are absent from previous and subsequent pyramids.

Dense edifice

If the Great Pyramid at Giza could be weighed, would it be heavier than every other building in the world?

Modern buildings do not compete with the Great Pyramid at Giza in Egypt in terms of mass. In fact, better materials and design have permitted skyscrapers to become less massive even as they have grown taller. For example, Chicago's Willis Tower (formerly the Sears Tower) weighs 223,000 tons, 142,000 tons less than the Empire State Building, which was built four decades earlier and is 200 feet (70 meters) shorter.

Designers of modern buildings are usually interested in maximizing internal space; consequently, buildings are up to 95 percent air on the inside. On the other hand, the Great Pyramid is nearly solid stone with the exception of two small burial chambers. Most descriptions of the Great Pyramid give its weight as six million tons.

However, according to *Guinness World Records*, the largest pyramid is actually the Quetzalcóatl Pyramid in Cholula, Mexico. Its volume is 4.3 million cubic yards, compared to 3.27 million cubic yards for the Great Pyramid at Giza.

Unable to find any estimates of the mass of the Quetzalcóatl Pyramid, I calculated it from the pyramid's volume and the density of the material it is made from—adobe. My rough calculation puts it at slightly less than the mass of the (granite, basalt, and limestone) Great Pyramid at Giza, making the latter the most massive building in the world.

Tiny toys

Today, websites for physics departments hardly mention simple mechanics and the simple machines that produce a mechanical advantage. I couldn't find any faculty members who conduct research in these areas. Much research has been done on miniaturization (micro machines, lab on a chip, etc.). Just as simple machines are applied on a "macro" scale, I bet there is just as much of an opportunity to employ them on a "micro" scale.

Classical mechanics is built on the foundations of Newton's laws of inertia, acceleration, action and reaction, and gravitation. It describes the motions of simple machines, such as levers, ramps, screws, pulleys, wheels, and axles, and the compound machines made from them. Therefore, a modern physicist would have difficulty securing funding to research the fundamental principles that govern the behavior of "macro" machines.

However, ongoing academic and industrial research in various fields is applied to making better machines. For example, materials science is an interdisciplinary field that brings together physicists, chemists, engineers, and even biologists, because some man-made materials are inspired by nature. New materials can be tailored for optimal performance, slower aging, and resistance to shear and other types of stresses.

The hubbub about "micro" machines (actually, most of it is about even smaller "nano" machines) is not the result of researchers hopping on a little bandwagon. Experiments in which researchers use an atomic-force microscope to probe molecular machines are analogous to experiments that were once used to develop fundamental laws of macroscopic mechanics. But the functioning of molecular machines is not analogous to that of big machines.

Unlike a large object rolling down an inclined plane, small particles in fluids experience significant drag and thermal fluctuations. Molecules are always in a state of random motion and are constantly colliding with each other. Electromagnetic interactions make molecules sticky. These factors throw a wrench in attempts to miniaturize machines. If it were possible to keep scaling down a macro machine, eventually, due to friction, random motion, and intermolecular interactions, it would stop working.

Yet molecular machines are a reality. As you read this, lots of protein motors are hard at work in your body, moving cargo within cells, beating the cilia in your windpipe, and contracting your muscles. Also, chemists have synthesized very simple molecular machines from smaller molecules. The development of more complex molecular machines will require advances in the understanding of these systems' chemistry and physics. The interesting outstanding questions about basic scientific principles, along with the availability of new tools for investigating the questions, fuel researchers' fascination with the tiny.

Twinkle, twinkle

One evening, I was walking through the house in the dark and was struck by how many little lights there were: clock radios, DVR, appliances, computers, surge protectors. I did a count and came up with 50 LED lights. How much energy will they use in a year, operating 24 hours a day?

The energy use of any device is its power consumption multiplied by how long it is on. The amount of power consumed by light-emitting diodes (LEDs) typically varies from less than a watt to a few watts, and it depends on the other elements in the circuit that draw power. For household LEDs, a good estimate is 0.5 watts per LED.

Therefore, energy used equals 50 LEDs times 0.5 watts per LED times 24 hours times 365 days. This comes out to 219,000 watt-hours, or 219 kilowatt-hours (kWh). According to my last electric bill, the cost per kWh, including taxes and other charges, was almost 14 cents. So the yearly cost of all those little lights is approximately $30.

Curly cords

Why do certain electrical cords (those used by fans, in particular) curl up over time? Certain others do not.

Most small household appliance cords have a jacket made of rubber or plastic, some varieties of which are cheaper and less durable than others. Rubber and plastic consist of long chain-like molecules called polymers. The number of bonds between the chains, which prevent them from sliding past each other, and the length of the chains, give a material its characteristic durability and flexibility.

Over time, pressure (bending), exposure to sunlight, temperature changes, and exposure to certain chemicals can cause the polymer molecules to become misaligned and/or to link, which deform and stiffen the cord jacket, respectively.

Mr. Weasley's collection

I just returned from a vacation, and I'm wondering how electrical utilization evolved such that the United States, England, and Europe implemented different outlet designs and voltage standards. How many different outlet designs and voltage standards are there in the world?

Enough different types of plugs are in use around the globe to make the plug-collecting hobby of Harry Potter's best friend's dad seem stimulating. *Electric Current Abroad*, a publication available from the U.S. Department of Commerce, lists 12 different plug types, but it says this list includes only those most commonly used.

Electricity was used primarily for lighting when it was introduced to households in the late 1800s. The first domestic appliances were plugged into light sockets. In the 1920s, the first two-prong plugs and sockets were manufactured, followed by three prong plugs and sockets. The third prong—the ground—is a safety feature. It disconnects the power supply by tripping a breaker or blowing a fuse in the event of a short circuit.

As electricity use in the home and office flourished, different countries came up with their own variations of the two- and three-prong plugs. Even in that pre-globalization era, efforts were undertaken to come up with international standards for plugs, but finding one that would fit with all existing installations was difficult.

The savvy globe-trotter can easily purchase an adaptor to plug into a strange-shaped outlet. But beware—an adaptor just makes it possible to get the plug into the wall. It does not change the line voltage to suit the appliance. Switching the voltage requires a converter or transformer.

Two basic voltage standards are used: the North American 110-120 volts and the European 220-240 volts. They arose as the electric power industry evolved simultaneously in Europe and North America. At that time, many countries were colonized by European powers, so the European standard is more common.

Nearly all countries use alternating current (AC). The first distribution system, designed by Thomas Edison, was direct current (DC). In the end, AC proved to be more practical, because it could be transmitted at higher voltages (and then stepped down to a lower voltage). This allowed smaller wires to be used for a given amount of power. The frequency of AC is 60 Hz (cycles per second) in some countries and 50 Hz in others. The frequency cannot be converted, and certain devices are sensitive to frequency.

Fortunately, many new electronic devices come with power supplies designed for use almost anywhere. Check the label for INPUT, which should list acceptable current type (AC or DC), voltage range, and frequency.

Electric synchrony

Electrical energy transmitted by wires has long been a staple of our economy. Alternating current is generated in three overlapping phases, with voltage stepped up by transformers for long-distance transmission. Multiple generators are synchronized so that the power phases are in consonance. Now we are adding wind and solar electrical power to our grids. How are these alternative energy sources created or adapted to be compatible with the power grids?

The steam turbines that produce most of the electricity in the United States generate alternating current (AC)—current that reverses direction many times per second. Most of the steam turbines are powered by the burning of fossil fuels, especially coal (nearly 50 percent of electricity generation) and natural gas (over 20 percent), or nuclear fission (nearly 20 percent). Steam is also produced by burning biomass materials, such as wood or waste, from geothermal resources in the Earth's crust, or by radiant heat from the sun.

Turbines are also driven by flowing or falling water—hydropower—which generates 6 percent of U.S. electricity, and wind, which is a small (1 percent) but growing source of energy. In some cases gears are used to maintain constant generator output in response to variable input. Otherwise, variable-speed generation turbines, including those driven by wind, must be linked to the grid through a device called an inverter that supplies code-compliant power.

Unlike AC produced by turbines, solar photovoltaic cells produce direct current (DC)—current that flows in one direction. An inverter converts DC into AC. If the system is connected to the grid, the inverter also synchronizes the current with the AC cycle on the grid. A basic inverter operates by running DC input to two switches that feed opposite sides of a transformer. The transformer converts direct current into alternating current when the switches are turned on and off rapidly.

In the case of distributed power generation—for example, individuals with photovoltaic systems that send excess power back to the grid—inverters also play a critical safety role. If the power on the grid is interrupted, the inverter switches to "island mode" so that no power is sent to the grid. This feature protects utility transmission line workers attempting to make repairs on the grid.

The existing grid was designed for centralized generation, and it cannot integrate distributed power generation on a large scale. To accelerate integration, the U.S. Department of Energy recently launched the Solar Energy Grid Integration Systems (SEGIS) research initiative. SEGIS aims to develop intelligent system controls that facilitate communication between utilities and distributed photovoltaic systems to improve energy management.

In chains

Why does California require the use of tire chains when you drive on snowy roads in winter? We stopped using tire chains in New England about 25 years ago.

Chains provide good traction but can damage roads. Some states ban chains, while others, like California, require them. I can think of three reasons California requires them:

1. The average Californian has less experience driving in the snow than those who grew up in the Great White North.
2. In California, most people do not put snow tires on their cars in the winter.
3. The snowy part of the state also happens to be mountainous, and the combination of unpredictable weather, steep grades, inexperience, and poor tires can spell disaster.

Equine engine

How close does a 1-horsepower engine relate to the power of an actual horse? Did they do actual measurements, or did they just adopt the term? Did they have steam engines before they had the term horsepower? If so, how did they define the power of those early engines?

James Watt is usually credited with introducing the term horsepower in the late 1700s to market his new steam engines. But just as Watt did not invent the steam engine (his rotative steam engines built on earlier pumping steam engines), he was not the first to compare engine power to a horse's power. Nearly a century earlier, Thomas Savery, who invented the first steam engine that approached commercial success, also stated the power of his engines in terms of the number of horses they could replace.

Between Savery's and Watts' time, the power of a horse was defined inconsistently by different engine makers. Watt estimated that the amount of weight a horse could pull over a given distance in a given period of time was 33,000 foot-pounds per minute, which has been the accepted definition of 1 horsepower ever since. Power is also now measured in watts, and 1 horsepower is equivalent to 746 watts.

Sources differ on how Watt came up with his definition of horsepower. Some say he based it on how quickly a draft horse could turn a mill wheel. According to another account, he based it on ponies lifting coal at a coal mine, but he increased the number by 50 percent to estimate the power of a horse, rather than that of a pony. Another source claims that Watt based it on the power of a horse but deliberately overestimated a horse's power by 50 percent so that he would not be accused of exaggerating the number of horses his engines could replace.

In pulling contests, draft horses have been observed to have a peak power output of nearly 15 horsepower for a few seconds. The average horse cannot work at a rate of 1 horsepower over long periods, but a fit draft horse can sustain 1 horsepower for hours.

Although the definition of horsepower was standardized more than two centuries ago, the method of measuring an engine's power has varied. For example, before the 1970s, American automakers measured and advertised their engines' gross power—the power at the engine's crankshaft with no belt-driven accessories. Since then automakers have quoted net horsepower—remaining power output after losses caused by standard power-consuming accessories.

Man's best friend v. 2.0

A group of dog fanciers has created a "new breed," the Labradoodle, by mating a Labrador with a poodle. How many generations would it take for the "breed" to breed true—that is, for a Labradoodle mated to a Labradoodle to produce a Labradoodle?

It depends on what characteristics (coat color and texture, height, bone structure) define a Labradoodle, and how much variation in each characteristic is considered acceptable.

As any parent knows, genetics can be surprising. For instance, two brown-eyed people can have a blue-eyed child. The gene for brown eyes is dominant—a child who inherits the gene for brown eyes from *either* parent will have brown eyes. The gene for blue eyes is recessive—a child needs copies of the gene from *both* parents to be blue-eyed.

As a dog breeder, it is easier to select for a recessive trait, because when a dog has that trait, one can infer its genetic makeup. When a dog has a dominant trait, it could carry two dominant genes for the trait, or the dominant gene and a recessive gene. In the latter case, descendents may crop up that have inherited two copies of the recessive gene. Deducing which ancestors were carrying that recessive gene, and eliminating the gene from the gene pool, may take many generations of crosses.

In practice, genetics is even more complicated. Usually more than two possible genes for a trait exist. Also, the activity of genes can be modified by other genes. For example, multiple genes interact to specify the color and shade of a dog's coat.

It took more than a quarter century for Boston terriers, black Russian terriers, and golden retrievers, breeds developed since the 1850s (recent enough for a somewhat reliable historical account), to breed true.

The process can be speeded up by increasing inbreeding, because breeding related dogs decreases the amount of variation in the gene pool. However, too much inbreeding can introduce genetic defects, such as decreased immunity and increased risk of cancer.

The Labradoodle originated in Australia in the 1970s or 1980s (accounts differ) as an attempt to produce a low-allergy guide dog for the blind. Labradoodles are not recognized as a breed by the American Kennel Club or other well-respected registries. The Labradoodle breed standard is currently too broad. For example, three categories of coat textures are recognized, ranging from a relatively flat Labrador-like coat to a curly poodle-type coat.

Taking to the sky

I read that the Wright brothers, who flew the first airplane, built their own engine, although at the time nobody knew how to build one and fire it up. There were no tools to make the hole for the piston, and so forth. Can you shed some light on this?

Charles Taylor, a talented machinist who worked in the Wright brothers' bicycle shop, built the engine for the 1903 Wright Flyer, generally considered the world's first powered airplane that actually flew. The engine was a 12-horsepower, four-cylinder internal-combustion model weighing 170 pounds.

Taylor purchased some of the parts he needed. The ignition switch came from the local hardware store. Parts that needed to be cast from molten metal were ordered from a foundry. Otherwise, Taylor used the tools in the Wrights' shop. For example, their lathe bored the holes for the pistons. The shop was set up for metalworking because when the Wrights were not refining their flying machines, they designed and built custom bicycles.

It took Taylor six weeks to make the engine. However, he did not invent the internal combustion engine. Such engines had been around for four decades and were being used in automobiles when the Wrights were building their Flyer. The Wrights wrote to a dozen automobile companies but could not find an engine that was sufficiently light and powerful.

The engine was very simple by today's standards. Gasoline was fed into the engine via gravity from a fuel tank attached to a wing. There was no carburetor and no spark plugs, and the engine tended to stall.

It is especially impressive that the Wright Flyer took to the sky while its main competition, Samuel Langley's Aerodrome, which had a considerably more powerful engine, failed. The Wrights' advantage stemmed from the very scientific approach they took toward designing an airplane.

Unlike other aspiring aviators of the time, the Wrights realized that they would need to control the airplane's pitch (up-and-down movement), yaw (side-to-side movement), and roll (rotation around an axis running the length of the plane). They built and tested a series of gliders beginning in 1899 and carefully noted the effects of each change they made. They even created their own wind tunnel to test small-scale models of different types of wings.

It took many crashes and improvements of their successive gliders before they felt ready to add a motor. Then, Taylor's motor, despite its limitations, permitted the Wrights to make history.

Off-kilter

When you hold up a carpenter's level, with the bubble in the middle, what is it level to? The Earth is round, so how can anything be level?

When the bubble is centered, the carpenter's level is parallel to a tangent to the Earth at that location. A tangent is a straight line that touches a sphere at just one point. It makes a 90-degree angle with the radius of the sphere at that point.

Since Earth is a bumpy sphere, the tangent is not always parallel to the ground itself. On a hillside, the tug of gravity is still toward the center of the planet, so the level is aligned when it is perpendicular to a line to the Earth's center.

Architecture by numbers

How were the ancient Romans able to engineer and build all their magnificent buildings using their unwieldy number system?

Roman architecture borrows both principles of design and methods of construction from the Greeks. However, it is the Romans' adoption of concrete as a standard technique of construction that revolutionized architecture. Concrete permits more imaginative design because it can be poured, and because it is strong enough to span vast distances.

Up until the last two centuries, structures were designed and built based on prior experience. A concept would be tried, and if it worked, variations of the concept might be employed for generations. Catastrophic failures were not uncommon, but architects and engineers learned from the failures and modified their designs accordingly.

The Romans used mathematics to design their buildings, particularly geometry and systems of proportions. However, only much more recently has mathematics been used to design buildings by taking into consideration the mechanical properties of the materials being used and the loads acting on a structure. These calculations require calculus, which was not developed until the 17th century.

Had the Romans needed more sophisticated mathematics to design their buildings, their number system might have been a constraint, but lifelong experience with Roman numerals would have made them seem a lot less cumbersome to them than they do to us.

2

Chemical concoctions

Sticky situations

I heard on some science TV show that no one knows for sure what makes glue work. Is this true? What does make glue stick? Does it depend on the type of glue? What do glues have in common?

We take sticky notes, glue sticks, Super Glue, and tape so for granted that it may come as a surprise that developing new adhesives is a very active area of research. Understanding what makes stuff sticky is key to making stickier adhesives or adapting them to new purposes.

Although people use the words glue and adhesive interchangeably, glues, which are made from natural materials, have been around a lot longer than adhesives, which are made from synthetic materials. According to archaeologists, ancient civilizations used sticky materials like tree sap to repair broken pottery as far back as 4000 B.C. Beeswax and tar were long used to seal gaps between planks in ships, and for centuries other glues have been made from fish, animal hides, and hooves.

White glues (adhesives), such as Elmer's, work by evaporation. As the water in Elmer's evaporates, the polyvinyl acetate latex that has spread into the crevices of the material being glued forms a pliable bond.

Super Glue has as its main ingredient a chemical called cyanoacrylate. The presence of water causes cyanoacrylate molecules to start linking with each other until they form a strong plastic mesh. Super Glue is all-purpose because pretty much everything has trace amounts of water on its surface.

Sticky notes are easily removable and restickable because the adhesive on the back of the notes consists of a thin, bumpy layer of microspheres. These little spheres stick to a surface, but the gaps between the spheres remain unstuck. In comparison to the pebbled appearance of the adhesive on the notes, the adhesive on tape looks flat and uniform under an electron microscope.

Even with synthetic sticky materials, scientists still have a thing or two to learn from Mother Nature. Geckos, with their amazing ability to run up walls, have been a recent source of inspiration. Geckos have about 500,000 microscopic hairs, called setae, on each foot. At the end of each seta are 1,000 branches tipped with pads called spatulae.

Unbalanced electrical charges around molecules in the spatulae and molecules in the surface to which the gecko is clinging interact, drawing the molecules together. These interactions, known as van der Waals forces, occur because electrons are mobile. At any instant, more electrons may be at one end of a molecule, giving that end a temporary negative charge, and the other end a temporary positive charge. This charge separation induces a movement of electrons in nearby molecules so that the charges fluctuate in synchrony, and the attraction is maintained over large numbers of molecules. Van der Waals forces, summed over the millions of spatulae in each foot, create a very strong bond.

Using this knowledge, researchers have developed a super-sticky material with "nanobumps" that resemble the spatulae on geckos' toes. If it could be mass-produced, this material could be made into reusable tape that even works underwater.

Strong bond

Why is the adhesiveness of white glues, such as Elmer's, stronger than that of glue sticks?

The sticky molecules in Elmer's all-purpose glue are mixed with water, which allows the glue to penetrate into tiny gaps on an object's surface. When the water evaporates, the sticky molecules remain behind and form many anchor points all over the surface. On the other hand, a glue stick glides over the pores and applies glue only to the bumps, resulting in fewer anchors.

The adhesive molecules in Elmer's and glue sticks are different, but they bond in similar ways (unlike Super Glue, which chemically reacts with water to form a highly interlinked mesh of molecules). However, the ingredients used to solidify a glue stick and help it glide over a surface reduce its adhesive strength.

Black gold

How do you get gasoline, kerosene, and other products from crude oil? Also, how is it possible to make gasoline from corn?

Crude oil, when recovered from an oil well, consists of a complex mixture of hydrocarbons—molecules made from hydrogen and carbon atoms. To make products of value from this mixture, hydrocarbons of different sizes are separated via distillation.

This involves heating crude oil to over 1,000 degrees Fahrenheit (540 degrees C) at the base of a fractionating column—a tower 260 feet (80 meters) high with a series of collecting trays at different heights. The hydrocarbon vapor cools as it moves up the column and condenses on the trays. Larger hydrocarbons condense on the trays near the base of the column, and smaller hydrocarbons condense on the higher plates.

Methane, ethane, propane, and butane (which have one, two, three, and four carbons, respectively) are collected from the very top of the column. They can be bottled and sold. Since they are odorless, smelly sulfur compounds are added for safety reasons.

The fractions condensing on lower trays include gasoline, kerosene, gas oil (used for diesel fuel and heating oil), and lubricating oil. The very large hydrocarbons that do not boil off are redistilled at low pressure to separate waxes, tar, and so on.

Subsequent processing steps depend on consumer demand. For example, to increase the yield of gasoline from crude oil, small hydrocarbons can be linked to form longer ones, and large hydrocarbons can be "cracked" into smaller ones. Hydrocarbons are also the starting materials for plastics, herbicides and pesticides, detergents, textiles such as acrylic and polyester, dyes, and cosmetics.

Gasoline, by the time you pump it into your vehicle, is a complex mixture of 200 chemicals added to improve performance and help fuel burn more cleanly. For instance, hydrocarbons of different lengths and structures are added to boost the fuel's octane rating. This reduces "knocking," which occurs when gasoline ignites spontaneously by compression, instead of by the spark from the spark plug.

In the past, tetraethyl lead was also added to reduce knocking. It was banned because of health risks and largely was replaced by methyl tert-butyl ether (MTBE). Now ethanol is replacing MTBE because of health concerns over the latter.

Ethanol is the fuel that is produced from corn or other starches or sugars. It is made in the same way as moonshine, by crushing and fermenting the grain, followed by distillation. Most engines can run on a mixture of up to 10 percent ethanol in gasoline, and "flexible fuel vehicles" can accommodate blends of up to 85 percent ethanol.

What's in a name?

Does it matter what brand of fuel you use in your car, insofar as engine performance and gas mileage are concerned?

Gasoline suppliers share pipelines, and different distributors fill up their tanks at the same terminals. Therefore, the gasoline itself is the same. The only difference between brands is the additives blended with the gasoline when it is loaded into tankers destined for a retail station. Major brands advertise that they use more or better-quality additives to control corrosion and the formation of deposits in the engine and fuel supply system.

However, an American Petroleum Institute representative was unaware of any independent testing that shows which brands are superior. In addition, since 1995, the U.S. Environmental Protection Agency has mandated the use of detergents in gasoline and has set performance standards to ensure that the detergents control engine deposits. Control of deposits enhances fuel economy and reduces pollutants in engine exhaust.

Under the Clean Air Act and its amendments, the composition of gasoline has undergone many changes. First was the phaseout of leaded gasoline. Average blood lead levels in the United States declined dramatically over the 15 years that the use of leaded gasoline dropped from its peak to near zero, reports the Centers for Disease Control and Prevention.

Later came the introduction, in the most polluted cities, of reformulated gasoline with more oxygen to increase fuel combustion. Oxygen content is increased through the use of oxygenates. Initially methyl tert-butyl ether (MTBE) was used, but due to health concerns it is being replaced by ethanol. Reformulated gasoline has lower levels of benzene, a known carcinogen, and other pollutants. Fuel reformulation is determined by federal and local mandates, rather than by brand.

Fuel reformulation is not the only factor responsible for reductions in pollutants. A decade-long study of tailpipe emissions, published in the journal *Environmental Science and Technology*, determined that reductions in three major pollutants—carbon monoxide, nitrogen oxides, and hydrocarbons—were mainly the result of improved onboard vehicle emission control systems. The researchers found similar emissions improvements in cities that mandated reformulated fuel and those that did not.

Since the composition of the different brands of fuel varies little, many companies have tried to attract consumers by advertising their green credentials. For the Sierra Club's environmental rankings of oil companies, see www.sierraclub.org/sierra/pickyourpoison.

Auto alternatives

As the world supply of fossil fuels dwindles, what alternatives to gasoline for vehicles are being researched or developed?

These days, the buzzword is biofuels—fuels derived from organic matter. The two most common biofuels are bioethanol and biodiesel. Bioethanol is made from starchy or sugary crops in the same process that yields homemade liquor. Yeast ferments sugar into ethanol, which is distilled to remove water. Biodiesel is made from vegetable oils or animal fats.

The United States has been ramping up production of ethanol from corn, but this cannot replace imported petroleum. Global corn prices have already increased as grain is being diverted from food chain to fuel tank. Corn is a difficult crop to grow, requiring high inputs of fertilizer and pesticides. According to some pessimistic estimates, it requires nearly as much energy to cultivate corn and convert it to ethanol as is obtained from the ethanol in the end.

On the other hand, there is a great deal of excitement about technologies to make ethanol from cellulose. Cellulose, the main structural component of plants, consists of long chains of sugars. An efficient process to convert cellulose into its component sugars would make feasible the production of ethanol from straw, crop waste, wood chips, and maybe even scrap cardboard and paper.

Hydrogen is another alternative source of energy for locomotion. Hydrogen can be burned or converted into electricity through fuel cells. Prototype hydrogen cars exist, but perversely, the hydrogen being used to power them is usually derived from natural gas. Hydrogen can be made by splitting water, but this requires a large input of energy. Storing and transporting hydrogen are also problems to be solved if hydrogen cars are ever to become practical.

Battery-powered electric vehicles are constantly improving. The major challenge in making them commercially viable is developing a battery that can power a vehicle for long distances, can be recharged repeatedly, and is not prohibitively expensive. The popular hybrid cars get around the limitations of batteries by combining gasoline power and electric power. Also, during braking, the electric motor in a hybrid car acts as a generator to recharge the batteries.

Hydrogen and batteries are essentially ways to store energy from other sources so that it can be used to move a vehicle. Other methods of energy storage are possible. For example, energy can be used to pump air into the pressurized tank of a compressed-air car. The expansion of air then moves the pistons in the engine. The car's emissions are clean, but, of course, the actual emissions depend on how the energy used to compress the air was produced. Prototype compressed-air cars exist, but research is ongoing to bring them from concept to market. The greatest challenge is creating a car that can achieve a useful driving range on a single tank of compressed air.

Sugar high

I have heard that sugarcane is five to ten times more efficient than corn in the production of ethanol. Is this true? If so, why isn't it being promoted?

Producing ethanol from sugarcane in Brazil is roughly seven times more efficient (with respect to the ratio of energy output to fossil fuel input) than producing ethanol from corn in the United States. However, more than this one statistic is needed to compare these two technologies.

Brazil's sugarcane ethanol program began 30 years ago during the oil crisis. The government adopted mandatory regulations on the amount of ethanol to be mixed with gasoline, and it subsidized ethanol production, mainly through taxes on gasoline. Now Brazil is the world's largest exporter of ethanol, and Brazilian ethanol is competitive with gasoline in international markets.

Sugarcane prefers warm climates, and in the United States the largest sugarcane producers are Florida, Louisiana, Hawaii, and Texas. American farmers also grow sugar beets in states with temperate climates. Currently, none of this sugar gets fermented into ethanol.

We eat all the sugar we produce, and we import another 20 percent of the sugar we consume. On average, each year every American gobbles down more than 40 pounds of refined sugar, nearly 45 pounds of corn-derived sweeteners, and just over a pound of honey and syrup. Annual per-capita sweetener consumption is the equivalent of about seven gallons of ethanol.

Because of the high cost of sugar in the United States, the domestic production of ethanol from sugar is not economically competitive with the production of ethanol from corn, according to data from the U.S. Department of Agriculture.

Brazil has an ideal climate for growing sugarcane, as well as low sugar prices. Despite these advantages, Brazil had a 15-year "learning curve" before its ethanol became cost-competitive with gasoline.

One reason for the efficiency of Brazilian sugarcane ethanol is that bagasse—the residue from sugarcane processing—is burned to provide heat for the distillation and electricity to run the machinery. Corn stover—stalks and leaves—could be used for this purpose, but it is not usually harvested.

The efficiency of corn-based ethanol could also be improved with the development of corn varieties that have higher starch content, or better enzymes to process the starch into sugar. In the meantime, the United States is protecting its corn-based ethanol industry with an import duty of 54 cents per gallon levied on Brazilian ethanol.

Both technologies raise concerns about the clearing of wild land for agriculture and the use of food to fuel vehicles.

Water fire

I received a video clip from a friend that deals with the use of water as an alternative to fossil fuels. Does this seem plausible to you? Neither of us can figure out why we haven't heard of this before. It seems too good to be true.

The water-as-fuel hype recurs periodically. For instance, an Indian chemist convinced his local government that he powered his scooter on fuel made by boiling herbs in water. Then there was Stanley Meyer's "water-powered car." An Ohio court ordered Meyer to repay investors after it found him guilty of "gross and egregious fraud."

One of the latest incarnations of water hype is a story on YouTube by a Cleveland-based television reporter about burning water. No, it is not the famous fire on Cleveland's once grimly polluted Cuyahoga River, which helped spur the environmental movement. The video shows clean saltwater going up in flames.

The demonstration is not a hoax, but saltwater won't reduce our dependence on other sources of energy. The adage "If it sounds too good to be true, it probably is" makes good sense. In order to burn, the water must be exposed to a strong, focused field of radio waves. When the field is turned on, the water burns. When it is switched off, the water stops burning.

In other words, unlike fossil fuels, water requires a constant input of energy to make it burn. No one has yet published an analysis that compares how much energy is recovered from burning the water versus how much is used to create the radio frequency field. However, it is impossible to extract net energy. It would violate the laws of thermodynamics and provide the basis for a perpetual-motion machine.

Water burns in the radio frequency field because it is being dissociated into hydrogen and oxygen, which are recombined by burning. The exact mechanism by which the field breaks bonds in water is under dispute, but the end result is similar to conventional electrolysis. Electrolysis uses an electric current to produce hydrogen and oxygen at separate electrodes, and more energy is used than is produced by burning the resultant hydrogen.

If using a radio frequency field to split water turns out to be more efficient than electrolysis, this new discovery could be of practical interest. Producing hydrogen from water is a way to store energy. If the sun is the source of energy to liberate hydrogen from water, the result is a clean-burning fuel produced by a renewable energy source.

Periodic-table personalities

Why are nuclear bombs so powerful? I know it has something to do with the splitting of an atom, but why does that cause such catastrophic damage?

There are two main types of nuclear bombs. In a fission bomb, large, unstable atoms (uranium or plutonium) split into smaller, more stable atoms. In a fusion bomb, also called a thermonuclear or hydrogen bomb, the nuclei of very small atoms combine to form larger, more stable atoms.

The binding energies that hold together the protons (positively charged particles) and neutrons (neutral particles) in the nucleus of an atom are approximately a million times stronger than the binding energies that hold together atoms in a molecule. Therefore, nuclear bombs are much more powerful than conventional bombs, in which chemical reactions—rearrangements of atoms in molecules—cause the explosion.

It might seem counterintuitive that opposite processes (splitting apart an atomic nucleus and fusing two nuclei) can both release energy. Whether fission or fusion releases energy depends on the size of the nucleus.

As atomic nuclei become larger, they grow more stable because of the strong nuclear force between nuclear particles. Atoms near iron (the 26th element) in the periodic table have the most stable nuclei. However, as atomic nuclei increase in size compared to iron, they become less stable, because there are more positively charged protons, which repel each other.

The more stable nuclei created by the fission of atoms larger than iron, or through the fusion of small atoms, have less mass than the original nuclei. The missing mass is transformed into energy, a process expressed mathematically by Einstein's famous equation $E=mc^2$.

Jolt-free beans

How is coffee decaffeinated?

The three main decaffeination processes are solvent decaffeination, decaffeination with carbon dioxide, and Swiss Water decaffeination. All three processes involve soaking the beans in chemicals to extract the caffeine.

Caffeine was first discovered and isolated in the late 19th century, and the first process to decaffeinate coffee, solvent decaffeination, was developed in Germany in 1900. The solvent is the liquid in which the coffee beans are soaked to remove the caffeine.

An ideal solvent removes the caffeine without removing compounds that give coffee its flavor and aroma. Many different (not always healthful) chemicals have been used to decaffeinate coffee, including alcohol, acetone, benzene, and methylene chloride, which was the preferred solvent until it was implicated in the depletion of the ozone layer. Ethyl acetate, a chemical that occurs naturally in some fruit, is now the preferred solvent.

In solvent decaffeination, the unroasted beans are steamed to make the beans more porous and the caffeine easier to extract. The beans are exposed to the solvent to dissolve the caffeine, and then they are rinsed, dried, and roasted.

Carbon dioxide decaffeination was patented in the early 1970s. In this method, carbon dioxide gas is compressed into a liquid at 50 times atmospheric pressure and is used as the solvent to extract caffeine. This method is particularly good at removing caffeine without removing flavor compounds, but a drawback is that it is expensive to build and maintain a carbon dioxide decaffeination plant. So the method is feasible for only large coffee producers.

Swiss Water decaffeination was patented in 1938 but was not commercialized until the late 1970s. In this process, coffee beans are soaked in hot water, which extracts the caffeine but also many of the flavor compounds. The water is passed through an activated carbon filter to remove the caffeine. Initially, the decaffeinated water was sprayed back on the beans after they had been partially dried to allow them to reabsorb the flavor compounds.

In the last 20 years, this procedure has been refined; now the caffeine-free water with the flavor compounds is used to remove caffeine from subsequent batches of beans. Since the water is already saturated with coffee flavor, the flavor compounds stay in the beans, but the caffeine is extracted.

Caffeine is one of many substances plants make to defend against insect attack. But the recent discovery of a caffeine-free variety of coffee related to commercially viable strains might ultimately permit plant breeding to render chemical decaffeination processes obsolete.

Decaf danger?

I was surprised to read about the chemicals once used in decaffeination, such as benzene, which I believe has been known (however, not really proven) to cause leukemia. Do I have the right chemical?

You are correct; benzene is a known carcinogen. Early efforts to decaffeinate coffee employed a number of other solvents now known or suspected to cause cancer, including chloroform, carbon tetrachloride, trichloroethylene, and methylene chloride.

In spite of this, even for those who were imbibing decaf before the newer methods of decaffeination started to emerge in the late 1970s, there is no evidence to suggest reason for alarm.

Only a very small amount of solvent (around one part per million) remains after the beans are rinsed and roasted. Methylene chloride, which was popular longer than the other solvents listed, appears to cause cancer in animals only when given in high doses (4,000 parts per million).

Also, studies that have compared decaf drinkers to those who drink regular brew have not shown an increased risk of cancer associated with drinking decaffeinated coffee.

Gently down the stream

There has been some coverage in the newspaper about a project of recycling wastewater in Southern California to make it drinkable again. If purifying wastewater is a lengthy and costly process, wouldn't it be cheaper to do the same thing with seawater? Add to that the mental-health aspects associated with the concept of drinking what used to be wastewater.

It may seem surprising, but according to the City of San Diego Water Department, it currently costs about twice as much to desalinate seawater as it costs to take the same quantity of water "from toilet to tap." The reason is that ocean water is about 25 times saltier than the starting point for recycled water.

Removing dissolved salts is the most energy-intensive step in producing drinking water. The more salt in the water, the more energy required to remove it. Salt removal is accomplished either via distillation or, more commonly, reverse osmosis. In reverse osmosis, water is pushed through a membrane that allows water molecules through, but not the dissolved salts.

According to a 2006 report by the Pacific Institute for Studies in Development, Environment and Security, the cost of desalinating water in California and delivering it to users may be as high as 1 cent per gallon and is unlikely to fall below one-third cent per gallon. Although considerably cheaper than bottled water, even the lower estimate is more than the price paid by most urban water users and is about 10 times the price paid by farmers in the western United States.

San Diego imports about 90 percent of its drinking water from Northern California and the Colorado River. As the costs of alternative sources of water rise due to drought and increased demand, desalination will become a more viable option. It already has in the Middle East, which is home to more than half of the world's desalination plants.

In the United States, direct recycling of wastewater to drinking water is not accepted practice, probably for the psychological reasons you mention. On the other hand, indirect recycling of wastewater into drinking water is common. For example, cities upstream discharge treated wastewater into rivers that serve as the drinking water supply for cities downstream. Also, in some places, including Los Angeles and Orange County, recycled water is used to top off underground aquifers that supply drinking water.

Recycled water does not contain levels of bacteria, heavy metals, or organic compounds that exceed drinking water standards. However, levels of dissolved salts are higher than those in the drinking water supply.

In San Diego, recycled water is used mainly for irrigation. Some new high-rises are being built with a dual plumbing system via which the city supplies recycled water for flushing toilets. The dual system adds around 10 percent to the cost of installing the plumbing.

Water, water everywhere

In this age of scientific wonders, is there any chance of someone finding a method of converting seawater into freshwater economically? If and when that happens, what will we do with all the salt?

As population growth increases the demand on existing sources of freshwater, desalination of seawater is becoming increasingly economically viable. The worldwide market for water desalination is increasing about 15 percent annually.

Reverse osmosis, which involves forcing seawater through a membrane that allows only water molecules through, is the most popular desalination technology in the United States. Improvements in the membrane material that make it longer-lasting and less likely to clog are increasing its cost-effectiveness. The concentrated salt solution that remains behind typically is dumped back into the ocean.

Several new desalination technologies are being explored. Freeze separation involves freezing seawater to get ice crystals of pure water. In vacuum distillation, saltwater is vaporized at low pressure, which requires less heat than distillation at atmospheric pressure. In electrodeionization, seawater passes between two parallel membranes on the inside of oppositely charged plates. Because ions in the seawater are attracted to the plates, the sodium, chloride, and other ions are pulled out through the membranes, leaving behind pure water.

Reticent rubber

Recently my neighbor remarked that he has always wondered why automobile tire wear dust, although it must add up to a significant amount, never builds up enough to be seen. I told him that I read somewhere that tire dust was eaten by bacteria specialized in that strange way. Is that a fact, or was it someone's imagination?

Tire particles do accumulate on the roadside and are washed away by rain. But it is also true that many kinds of bacteria and fungi degrade rubber. Natural latex rubber, which is produced by more than 2,000 species of plants to protect their wounds while they heal, consists of long chains of carbon atoms. Rubber-degrading microbes break down the chains using specialized enzymes. Recently some of these enzymes have been identified and the DNA sequence of the corresponding genes determined.

Three-quarters of all natural rubber harvested is used to make automobile tires. Softness and flexibility are ideal for nature's bandage for trees, as well as products made from it, such as rubber bands, gloves, and protection for other body parts. However, tires must be more durable. Therefore, tires are made using variations of the vulcanization process invented by Charles Goodyear in 1839.

Vulcanized rubber is produced by heating natural or man-made rubber with sulfur and other chemicals. During the process, sulfur bridges form between the rubber's carbon chains. Microbes have difficulty gaining access to the linked chains in vulcanized rubber. Vulcanized rubber is also a less hospitable environment to microbes, because it is less permeable to gases and water than natural rubber. Furthermore, some of the chemicals added during the vulcanization process are toxic. As a result, biodegradation of rubber, especially vulcanized rubber, is a very slow process.

Because scrap tires represent 12 percent of all solid waste, there is considerable interest in optimizing rubber biodegradation. Currently about half of waste rubber is combusted to generate electricity, or ground up and used in asphalt mixtures for road resurfacing. Vulcanized rubber can also be recycled by mixing fine particles of it with newly produced, nonvulcanized rubber, but the performance characteristics of recycled rubber are not optimal.

Recent research has shown that higher-quality recycled rubber can be produced by pretreating vulcanized rubber with bacteria that break sulfur bridges between carbon chains, which frees the carbon chains to form new links. Because researchers have discovered microbes specialized to cut carbon chains, microbes specialized to break sulfur bridges, and microbes that can detoxify vulcanized rubber, they are now exploring multistep approaches to bioremediation of tires.

On top of Old Smoky

Inside casinos I can see no cigarette smoke, but when I leave, my clothes smell like smoke. I then conclude I've been exposed to secondhand smoke. Am I wrong?

You are probably correct, because the thousands of chemicals in cigarette smoke give it a very recognizable smell. Assuming that no one is smoking inside the building, it is possible that people are smoking outside, near the air intake openings.

It would not take much smoke for you to be able to detect it. One study showed that about 3,000 cubic meters of fresh air (equivalent to the volume of about 10 spacious living rooms) is needed to sufficiently dilute the smoke from one cigarette to protect against eye and nose irritation. Also, the many fibers in fabric provide a large surface area to which smoke molecules can cling, so clothes tend to pick up the smell of smoke quite easily.

Odor eater

Baking soda does a remarkable job of neutralizing foul odors. How does it work?

Many unpleasant odors, such as those associated with vinegar, sour milk, and rotten eggs, are acidic molecules. Baking soda—sodium bicarbonate—is a weak base that can react chemically with acids to neutralize them. It can also react with a stronger base, so baking soda also neutralizes the basic molecules that cause fishy or ammonia smells.

The reaction between the baking soda and odor molecules is not visible, because not many molecules react at once. However, you can see the reaction if you mix vinegar and baking soda. The gas that bubbles off is carbon dioxide, which is formed during the reaction. This is the reason you may burp when you take antacids. Antacids are usually made of calcium carbonate, but their reaction with stomach acids is similar to the vinegar/baking soda reaction.

Exquisite earth

What exactly is terra preta, and what does it have to do with reducing global warming?

Terra preta is Portuguese for "dark earth." It is a carbon-rich, highly fertile soil that covers as much as 10 percent of the Amazon Basin, an area as large as France. *Terra preta* is also found in other, mostly tropical, regions. Archaeologists used to think that this black soil was deposits from ancient volcanoes or pond bottoms. However, chemical analyses of the soil, as well as the consistent presence of broken pottery, have led most researchers to conclude that the soil is the result of human activity.

The indigenous people of the Amazon Basin, who must have been more numerous than once supposed, began the deposition of *terra preta* nearly 2,500 years ago, according to carbon dating. The darkest soils seem to contain a mixture of waste from human settlements. Incorporated into the slightly lighter surrounding soils are large quantities of charred organic matter, or char. Good char is produced not by slash-and-burn agriculture, but by plant matter smoldered slowly in a low-oxygen environment.

Crops grown in *terra preta* are twice as productive as those grown in nearby unaltered soil. The soil in the Amazon region typically is too poor to support sustainable agriculture. It is acidic, low in nutrients, and high in aluminum, which makes it toxic to soil microbes. Char reduces the soil's acidity, makes the aluminum ions less reactive, and increases the soil's capacity to retain nutrients. One study found that the bacterial diversity in *terra preta* was 25 percent greater than that in adjacent unaltered soil.

Ancient farmers were surely not thinking about global warming when they incorporated char into the soil, but it is a remarkably effective method to sequester carbon dioxide. Plants sequester carbon dioxide as they grow because they use it as a building block for the molecules that constitute wood. Unfortunately, when plants die and decompose, the carbon dioxide is released back into the atmosphere. In contrast, the black carbon from the char added by ancient farmers has remained in the soil for millennia.

Calculations by some researchers suggest that the creation of new *terra preta* could store more carbon each year than is emitted by all of current fossil fuel use. Efforts to incorporate char into large-scale farming are under way. One company has developed a contraption that converts farm waste into biofuel while producing char. But scientists do not yet have all the dirt on the ancient farmers' tricks, such as what is the right type of char for each soil type.

Drug disintegration

Why does the effectiveness of vitamins, minerals, and medicines degrade over time? According to a pharmacist I asked, freezing does not keep them viable. Why not?

Freezing preserves food by interfering with microbial activity. But decay due to microbes is not the main problem for most medicines and nutritional supplements. Instead, over time, chemical reactions cause the degradation of the drug substance, the nondrug ingredients, or even the container, which may then leach chemicals into the medicine.

Reaction with oxygen in air (oxidation) and reaction with water (hydrolysis) are especially common modes of breakdown. Exposure to light, heat, and high humidity can increase the rate of drug decomposition. Accordingly, the bathroom medicine cabinet is a bad place to store medicine.

At least 90 percent of a medicine's original potency must remain prior to its expiration date. Estimates of a medicine's shelf life are based on standard conditions, but breakdown may be faster or slower, depending on the storage conditions. Breakdown products can be toxic, and their identity can vary depending on how the medicine is stored.

Proper disposal of unused medicines is critical because drugs are now widespread in waterways. Even if their concentrations are too low to affect humans, they may affect fish and other wildlife, and residues of antibiotics might encourage the development of drug resistance in bacteria. Unless your municipality has a pharmaceutical take-back location, the Environmental Protection Agency recommends disposing of medicines in the trash after mixing them with an undesirable substance such as kitty litter.

Lone nutrients

How are individual vitamins extracted or manufactured to put into pills or food supplements?

The first vitamin discovered, thiamin, was isolated at the beginning of the 20th century by soaking brown rice in water and separating the compound that dissolved. Nutritional compounds are still extracted from plant parts by bathing them with different liquids, such as alcohol, hydrocarbons, or water, and then distilling the resulting solution. The type of liquid selected for the extraction depends on the vitamin's structure and whether it is water-soluble or fat-soluble.

It is cheaper to make vitamins than to extract them. Therefore, nearly all vitamins available commercially are manufactured. They are produced either through a series of complex chemical reactions perfected by chemists or by microorganisms that have been engineered to churn out large quantities of individual vitamins. They may also be made by a partnership of chemists and microbes, as in the case of vitamin C.

Vitamin C is produced in larger quantities than any other vitamin because, in addition to its use as a supplement, it is added to some cosmetics and is employed by the food industry to prevent the discoloration of food pigments. More than 100,000 tons of vitamin C is made annually. Most vitamin C producers use the Reichstein process, which dates to 1933. It transforms glucose into vitamin C in four steps, the first of which is accomplished by bacteria, and the subsequent three by chemists.

Vitamin B12 has a considerably larger and more complicated structure than vitamin C. The chemical synthesis of vitamin B12 involves about 70 steps, which makes it too technically challenging and expensive for industrial-scale production. Vitamin B12 cannot be extracted from plants either, because plants do not make it. However, many bacteria make vitamin B12 to catalyze reactions involved in fermentation. Genetically engineered bacterial strains that provide high yields of vitamin B12 are responsible for the more than 10 tons of vitamin B12 produced commercially each year.

Vitamin deficiencies were a pervasive health problem worldwide at the turn of the 20th century. In developed nations, programs established in the mid-20th century to fortify processed foods with vitamins have largely alleviated vitamin deficiencies. However, in developing nations, food processing and distribution are limited, and many staple crops, including corn, rice, and cassava, lack several vitamins. One approach to this problem is biofortification—breeding or engineering plants to produce additional vitamins. Progress has been made with biofortification of vitamin E, folate (vitamin B9), and beta-carotene (which our bodies can convert to vitamin A).

Rub-a-dub-dub

I know that soap in the 19th century was made from animal fat. How does a bar of soap made today differ from that made with animal fat? And how did early people bathe before they had soaps made from animal fat?

The earliest accounts of soap-making date from 2800 B.C., but the process seems to have been independently discovered by many different civilizations and may have been known even in prehistoric times. However, soap was initially used for purposes other than bathing, such as to prepare wool for dyeing.

Some early cultures did emphasize personal cleanliness, including the Romans and the Greeks, who rubbed themselves with fine sand and oil and removed the mixture with a metal instrument called a strigil.

Soap consists of linear molecules with an electric charge on one end, which can be created by treating animal fat with a strong base (such as lye). The charged end of the soap molecule is attracted to water. The neutral end is repelled by water and combines with oil. These properties allow soap (old-fashioned and modern) to help oil and water mix.

Soap-making was an established craft in Europe by the late 17th century. Soaps from southern France, Spain, and Italy, made from olive oil, were particularly renowned for their quality. However, soap was heavily taxed and thus considered a luxury item.

Until the mid-19th century, most American colonists, particularly those in rural areas, made their own soap by boiling lye extracted from wood ash with tallow—animal fat—which they saved all year. Because it was difficult to get the concentration of the lye just right, this method produced inconsistent results.

The first key advance in soap-making was the invention, in the late 18th century, of a more reliable method of producing a strong base.

The second key advance was the development, during World War I, of detergents. Detergents are made from petroleum, and detergent molecules can be tailored to have specific properties. For example, although soap binds with the calcium ions found in hard water and produces soap scum, detergents can be made that do not bind with calcium.

Many of today's soaps are actually detergents, or a mix of detergents with soap derived from vegetable oils or animal fats, with added fragrances, moisturizers, and vitamins.

The plethora of cleansing products available and our modern obsession with personal cleanliness can be traced back to an advertising campaign for Lifebuoy soap, begun in the 1930s, that coined the term B.O.

Chore tech

How come I can use cold water in my washing machine but I have to use hot water in my dishwasher?

The reformulation of laundry detergents over the last few decades has made it possible to wash clothes in cold water and still get them clean. People traditionally have washed clothes in hot or warm water, but the increasing popularity of synthetic fabrics and the desire to reduce household energy consumption have fueled a trend toward cooler wash temperatures.

Fabrics get stained or dirty in three ways: Dirt gets physically trapped between the fibers, electrical attractions hold together the dirt and fabric molecules, or a chemical reaction occurs between a dirt compound and the fabric to form a new compound. In the latter situation, hot water may make a stain permanent by stimulating the chemical reaction. Otherwise, hot water makes it easier to separate dirt molecules from the fabric, because molecules jiggle around more when they are warmer.

Critical to the cold-water effectiveness of modern detergents is the inclusion of enzymes that chop up dirt molecules. The four major classes of detergent enzymes are proteases, lipases, amylases, and cellulases. Proteases work on protein-based stains such as grass, egg, and blood. Lipases work on fats and oils. Amylases remove starch-based stains such as potatoes, gravy, and baby food. Cellulases smooth the surface of cotton fabrics by cutting off the fuzz and tiny fibers generated by wear and washing.

Surfactants have also been modified to enhance cold-water laundering. Surfactants loosen dirt from fabric and suspend it in the wash. Like soap, they are molecules with a hydrophilic (water-loving) tail and a hydrophobic (water-hating) head. When the hydrophobic ends of a bunch of surfactant molecules glom on to greasy grime, they form micelles—tiny oil blobs dissolved in water thanks to the outward-pointing hydrophilic tails of the surfactant. Cold-water surfactants have heads that are extra-hydrophobic to help them better interact with oil, which dissolves more poorly in cold water.

Dishwasher detergent has also been reformulated to enhance cleaning and make it less harsh on dishes. Of course, dishwashers do not rely on agitation to help remove cooked-on food. Even more important, hot water helps destroy bacteria and viruses that could cause food-borne illnesses.

Hot water is still used for laundry when there is a risk of disease transmission, such as for hospital and hotel linens, but for the most part, high-tech suds allow us to save energy and preserve our favorite duds.

3

Body parts

Toe the line

Why do some people, like me, have second toes that are longer than their big toes? Is it a genetic specificity? Is it a characteristic that occurs more in women than in men, or more in particular ethnic groups?

You are in good company. The Statue of Liberty has short big toes, or what is referred to as the Greek foot. Lady Liberty's sculptor, Frédéric Auguste Bartholdi, was trained in the classical tradition, and Greek and Roman statues often have short big toes. Leonardo da Vinci drew skeletons with Greek feet, rather than so-called Egyptian feet, in which the big toe is longest.

Some cultures have considered short big toes to be a sign of intelligence. (Disclaimer: I have Greek feet.) Unfortunately, Greek feet got a bad rap when, in 1927, a doctor named Dudley Morton published a paper describing a foot disorder associated with short big toes.

According to Morton's findings, the head of a short big toe cannot readily reach the ground and therefore does not carry its full share of the body's weight. As a result, the second toe carries extra weight. Calluses develop on the ball of the feet beneath the second and third toes, and tenderness may develop in this area.

However, a study of more than 3,500 men enlisted in the Canadian Army during World War II revealed absolutely no relationship between toe length and distribution of weight on the foot or foot pain. The researchers concluded that feet develop ways to compensate for variants in structure.

The reason for the discrepancy between these findings and Morton's may be that the vast majority of patients who came to see Morton complaining of foot pain caused by "Morton's Toe" were women. Women are more likely to wear high-heeled shoes, which compound the problem by forcing the weight toward the front of the foot.

Researchers have reported varying incidences of Greek feet in different populations, ranging from 3 percent to 40 percent. Extreme cases, where the big toes are less than two-thirds the length of the second toes, are rare. The trait is thought to be genetic, with Greek feet being recessive and Egyptian feet being dominant.

Gender differences in the relative lengths of fingers and toes are small. Nearly all of the research on gender differences in digit length has focused on the ratio of the lengths of the index and ring fingers. Studies indicate that minor differences in this ratio, possibly caused by exposure to hormones in the womb, are associated with certain personality traits, susceptibility to disease, and even sexual orientation. These claims are controversial, because research in many areas of human health and behavior has shown that most traits are a result of complex interactions between nature and nurture.

Surgeons' favorite organ

If the appendix is a relatively useless organ in our bodies, why do we have it? Did the appendix used to have a purpose in the bodies of early man?

Someone once said that the only function of the appendix is financial support of the surgical profession. About 7 percent of the population in developed countries will suffer from appendicitis in their lifetime, but appendicitis seems to be rare in undeveloped countries. It is unclear if diet or some other factor contributes to this difference.

In humans, the appendix is a wormlike pouch, three-and-a-half inches long on average, attached to the first part of the large intestine. In herbivorous mammals, such as rabbits, a much larger analogous structure houses bacteria that help break down cellulose, a large plant molecule. The appendix is present in many vertebrates, including other primates.

The human appendix does not contain cellulose-digesting bacteria, so humans cannot digest cellulose (which is why lettuce is roughage). Therefore, the appendix is often called a vestigial organ—a structure that has become diminished in size and lost its original physiological function.

That does not mean the human appendix has no function. Of the many functions hypothesized, a role in immunity is considered the most likely, although this remains controversial. The appendix, along with other parts of the digestive system, produces immune system cells, which can respond to ingested, disease-causing microbes. Whether the appendix contributes significantly to the immune response is unknown, since the lack of an appendix does not cause any obvious health problems.

Longer and longer

How can your nails continue growing throughout your life? How are they formed?

The first sign of nail formation occurs at week 10 of prenatal development, when a thickened area of skin called the primary nail field appears at the tip of each finger. The nail fields burrow into the skin, and the side and lower borders become thickened to form nail folds. The cells in the bottom nail fold continue to divide to produce the nail.

The fingernails reach the tips of the fingers by the end of the eighth month of pregnancy. The toenails, which begin development later than the fingernails, reach the tips of the toes just before birth. The extent of nail growth can be used as an indicator of how prematurely a baby has been born.

Most of what we can see of our nails is tightly packed layers of dead cells that are full of a tough protein called keratin. Keratin is also an important component of hair, feathers, beaks, horns, hooves, and the outermost layer of skin.

As new cells are produced in the nail's germinal matrix (base or root), which is located under the skin behind the fingernail, they are pressed forward and upward into the nail. They die, but remain firmly attached to their neighbors to create the solid nail. As the nail streams along the nail bed, new cells produced in the bed are added to it, helping compensate for surface wear.

Tough tips

What purpose do toenails and fingernails serve?

They serve as mini body armor to protect the tips of our fingers and toes. Of course, fingernails also come in handy for scratching itchy spots and picking up small objects. A less obvious, but important, function of fingernails is to enhance the sensation in the fingertip.

When we use our fingertips to feel something, the nail acts as a counterforce. It increases the compression of the sensory organs between the pad of the finger and the nail, which makes us better able to distinguish fine detail on the surface we are touching.

Ashes to ashes

When a person is cremated, how much do the ashes weigh? Is there anything that doesn't burn?

The weight of the cremains (cremated remains) depends on several factors: the temperature of the cremator furnace and the duration of the cremation, and the individual's weight, height, age, and gender. On average, the cremains of a fully developed adult weigh 5 pounds (2.3 kilograms), or approximately 3.5 percent of body weight. The range is from around 2 pounds to 8 pounds.

Cremains are not really ashes. Most of what remains after cremation is bone, often sizeable fragments. The larger and heavier a person's skeleton is, the greater the weight of his or her cremains. As a result, the cremains of men are 2 pounds heavier on average than the cremains of women. Also, the cremains of older adults are lighter on average than those of younger adults because bone density decreases with age.

The chemical composition of cremains is mainly calcium and phosphate—the major constituents of bone. Smaller amounts of carbon, potassium, sodium, chloride, magnesium, iron, and other minerals also remain. Melted metal from dental fillings and surgical implants, such as artificial hip joints, is usually removed, and the cremains are pulverized to give them the consistency of coarse sand.

Holey lids

When I was inserting my contact lenses, I noticed a tiny hole on the inside corner of my bottom eyelids. What are these holes?

They are called puncta and are the openings to the tiny canals through which tears drain. Tears flow from these canals into a tear sac and then down the tear duct into the nose. In fact, you can taste eyedrops after they flow from the puncta into your nose and drip onto the back of your tongue.

Producing peepers

When a human is developing, how are the eyes formed?

We start out as a ball of indistinguishable, genetically identical cells. A cell in what becomes the eye is different from a muscle cell or skin cell because it makes different proteins—the cell's workhorses. For example, proteins called crystallins pack the lens of the eye and help focus light onto the retina.

During development, chemical signals released by other cells and physical contacts with other cells can tell a cell to switch on certain genes, thereby making it produce certain proteins. A gene called PAX6 is a master gene that initiates eye development. The same gene initiates eye development in fruit flies, and if researchers activate PAX6 randomly, flies end up with eyes in unusual places.

Eye formation begins in a 22-day-old human embryo. At this stage, the brain and head are tube-shaped and consist of sheets of cells. Outward bulges form in an inner sheet of cells. When these bulges—called optic vesicles—contact the outer sheet of cells, the formation of the eye's lens is initiated. As the optic vesicles grow outward, their base narrows to form a stalk. This stalk eventually forms the optic nerve.

The side of the optic vesicle opposite the stalk pushes inward to become bowl-shaped, with the developing lens at its center. After many rounds of cell division, cell migration, and cell death, the layers of tissue making up the bowl behind the lens become the retina, with its ordered arrangement of light-sensitive rod and cone cells, supporting cells, and nerve cells that send electrical impulses to the brain.

A small opening, the pupil of the eye, remains in the bowl of the optic vesicle. The iris—the colored part of the eye, which is a muscle that expands and contracts the pupil—develops from the tissue in the optic vesicle that surrounds the future pupil.

The cornea, eyelids, and other parts of the eye develop in similar ways, with signals from other cells being paramount in switching on the appropriate genes for cells to take on the correct identity.

Both optic vesicles begin from a single patch of cells. Activation of a gene called sonic hedgehog (scientists have a lot of fun naming genes) is necessary for the splitting of this patch of cells so that two optic vesicles form. A mutation in the sonic hedgehog gene can result in cyclopia, a single eye in the center of the face. Infants born with cyclopia do not survive past birth because the condition is accompanied by brain defects.

Guardian lashes

What is the purpose of the lashes on your lower eyelid?

Their function is partly cosmetic—to frame those baby blues (or greens or browns)—but they also help protect the eye. They can deflect dust, foil insects, and shield the eye from reflected sunlight. If you gently touch the tips of your upper or lower lashes, you will see how exquisitely sensitive the nerves at the base of the lashes are to the deflection of the lashes. Because the lashes project outward, they trigger a protective blink reflex when an object comes too close to your eye.

Stopping short

Why don't eyelashes grow beyond a certain length, unlike the hair on one's head?

Some people who want thicker eyelashes have hair follicles from their scalp transplanted onto their eyelids. The transplanted hairs act like head hairs. They keep growing and require trimming.

Within each hair follicle (a pit containing the hair) is a biological "clock" that determines speed of hair growth and how long the hair grows before it falls out. Unfortunately for folks hoping for more hair on their heads, or less on their backs, the exact genes and molecules responsible for the hair cycle clock are still an enigma.

Grating habit

What happens when you crack your knuckles/joints? Is it bad for you?

Different parts of a joint—ligaments, tendons, cartilage, and synovial fluid—can snap, crackle, and pop for different reasons.

Ligaments connect bone to bone to strengthen the joint. Tendons connect muscle to bone and move the bone by transmitting the force created by the muscle. When a joint moves, cracking noises are created by the loosening and tightening of ligaments, as well as the change in position of tendons and their snapping back into place. Such noises are normal and are especially common in the knee and ankle joints.

On the other hand, grinding cartilage is a sign of an arthritic or injured joint. Smooth cartilage coats the ends of the bones that come together to form the joint. A joint capsule containing a lubricant surrounds the cartilage surfaces.

In a normal joint, the lubricated cartilage surfaces glide past each other with less friction than a skate on ice. Unfortunately, cartilage has very little ability to repair itself. Worn cartilage can make noise as it grates together. Loose pieces of cartilage can even break off and get caught in the joint, causing it to lock.

Some people can pop their knuckles by pulling on their fingers, which increases the space in the joint capsules. This reduces the pressure on the synovial fluid—the lubricant in the joints. Synovial fluid contains dissolved gases (carbon dioxide, oxygen, and nitrogen). Like the bubbles of gas that form when a bottle of sparkling water is opened, the reduced pressure on the synovial fluid can cause a bubble of gas to pop into existence. The bubble can be seen on an X-ray and takes approximately 20 minutes to redissolve in the synovial fluid.

Microphones on a knuckle detect two separate sounds when the joint is cracked. One is the sound of the gas bubble forming. The other is probably the sound of the joint capsule (which would be pulled inward slightly as the pressure in the joint decreased) snapping back into place because the formation of the gas bubble increases the pressure within the capsule.

Habitual knuckle crackers are not more likely to develop arthritis, but they are more likely to experience minor swelling and have poorer grip strength. However, the researchers who reported these findings pointed out that they do not prove knuckle cracking causes these problems. Only some people can crack their knuckles. It is possible that these people have looser ligaments to begin with, and the looser ligaments may predispose them to hand weakness and swelling.

Local harvest

What type of tissue would be used if stem cells were harvested from an adult?

Many adult tissues have stem cells, including the skin, gut, respiratory tract, liver, muscle, and brain, where they play a role in tissue repair and renewal. Not all of these stem cells are amenable to being harvested and transformed into other cell types.

Many studies have employed hematopoietic stem cells, which are found in bone marrow and generate all the types of cells in the blood. They have been used to treat blood disorders for three decades, and under the right conditions they can be coaxed to give rise to many other cell types.

Recently, researchers discovered stem cells in fat and have transformed them into other tissue types. It would be ideal if stem cells from fat prove to be as versatile as those from bone marrow. Liposuction is simpler than removing bone marrow, and even slender people carry a large-enough fat supply for their own treatment.

Cell selection

Embryonic stem cell research is controversial in many countries. Does adult stem cell research hold the same therapeutic promise(s)?

The jury is still out. Depending on who you ask, you will be told either that adult stem cells have demonstrated a surprising ability to transform into other cell types and repair damaged tissue, or that such transformations are relatively rare and can sometimes be accounted for by alternative explanations.

Embryonic stem cells are taken from three- to five-day-old embryos. These cells are exciting to researchers because at this stage, they have the potential to give rise to any cell type (muscle, bone, nerve, skin). On the other hand, it was initially thought that adult stem cells—which are found in many tissues (in children and adults), as well as umbilical cord blood and the placenta—could produce only progeny cells corresponding to their tissue of origin. For example, skin stem cells give rise to the various types of cells in the skin.

However, many recent studies suggest that adult stem cells can generate cell types other than those in their tissue of origin. Researchers coax stem cells into taking on a specific identity by selectively exposing them to chemicals that cells normally use to communicate with each other. Coaxing cells to take on a specific identity and verifying that they have indeed taken on that identity is technically challenging, and many studies have proven difficult to replicate.

Preliminary results of efforts to develop adult stem cell treatments do provide reason for optimism. For example, a few small human trials have shown that injecting adult stem cells into the blood stream can lead to some improvement in heart function after bypass surgery. But scientists still have much to learn about both embryonic and adult stem cells before clinical therapies live up to their promise.

If adult stem cell research advances to the point where scientists can consistently generate large numbers of cells of the tissue of interest, adult stem cells have three potential advantages over embryonic stem cells. First, ethical controversy has arisen over the destruction of embryos to obtain stem cells. Second, more research is needed to overcome the risk that rapidly dividing embryonic stem cells could lead to tumors. Third, using a patient's own adult stem cells in a treatment would overcome the issue of immune rejection.

Whiter shade of pale

Why don't some scars tan?

The most obvious possible explanation is that the scar tissue has fewer melanocytes—cells that produce the dark pigment melanin—than the surrounding skin. However, this does not appear to be the case.

In one study, researchers took biopsies from old, pale scars and from the adjacent normal skin of Caucasian volunteers. The researchers were surprised to discover that the number of melanocytes was about the same in scar tissue and nonscar tissue. In addition, the amount of melanin appeared to be similar in the scarred and normal skin.

The researchers proposed two hypotheses to explain why scars may appear pale even though melanocytes are present and appear to be functioning normally. First, scar tissue may have fewer blood vessels, resulting in decreased blood flow and whiter skin. Second, the structural properties of scar tissue can cause it to reflect light differently than normal skin.

In normal skin, fibers of the structural protein collagen are randomly oriented. As a result, skin scatters light in random directions. When skin is injured, the interwoven arrangement of collagen is destroyed. In an effort to repair the damage as quickly as possible, the body lays down new collagen fibers in linear strips parallel to each other. The scar reflects light mainly along a direction perpendicular to the skin.

Also, the upper layer of the skin over the scar may be thinner and may absorb less light. Thus, the scar may reflect more light toward the observer and appear whiter.

Healing potion

How does vitamin E lotion help scars?

Since vitamin E was found to be a major antioxidant in skin, physicians have recommended that patients apply it to injured skin to reduce scarring. Antioxidants mop up free radicals—highly reactive molecules that are produced at the site of a wound. Free radicals can damage cells and can also interfere with the production of collagen. Therefore, vitamin E should protect skin and promote healing.

Yet, despite its popularity, there is little scientific evidence that vitamin E reduces scarring. In fact, some studies have found the opposite. In one carefully designed study, published in *Dermatologic Surgery* (April 1999), patients applied a regular ointment (Aquaphor) to one side of a surgical wound and the same ointment mixed with vitamin E to the other side of the wound. In the majority of cases (90 percent), vitamin E had no effect or actually worsened the scar's appearance. Also, about one-third of patients developed a rash on the vitamin-E-treated skin.

Replacement parts

How can I donate an organ to give someone else a chance at a longer life?

Lack of donor organs is a big problem in the United States, where more than 100,000 people are on waiting lists, and 19 people die each day while waiting for an organ, according to the official U.S. government website for organ and tissue donation (www.organdonor.gov). Some countries, including France, Spain, and Belgium, have solved the problem of lack of organ donors by adopting "opt out" policies. This means that everyone is considered a potential donor when they die unless they have said otherwise. Typically only about 2 percent of people choose to opt out.

In the United States, you must "opt in" to be considered as an organ donor. You can request an organ donor card at the Department of Motor Vehicles, or download one from the Donate Life website at www.donatelife.net. The argument against an opt-out system has to do with informed consent. Silence is not consent, because if people do not know about the policy, they cannot opt out. Therefore, an opt-out policy raises ethical questions but, of course, so does the current opt-in policy and the resulting chronic donor shortage.

You can also become a "living donor" and donate a kidney, partial liver, lung, or partial pancreas. Medical costs are paid through the organ recipient's insurance, but the donor is not compensated for taking time off from work. More information is available on the Donate Life website. To learn about becoming a bone marrow donor, see www.marrow.org or contact your local blood bank.

Not so wise

What is Nature's purpose for wisdom teeth?

Wisdom teeth were the greatest thing before sliced bread. The extra surface area they provide is handy for chewing nuts, coarse grains, and raw meat. In other words, they helped our long-lost ancestors extract more calories from tough stuff. As humans have found ways to make food more toothsome, wisdom teeth have become disadvantageous, except to surgeons who make a living extracting them.

Our jaws are considerably smaller than those of our ancient ancestors. It is often impossible to squeeze in an extra set of molars, and the resulting prevalence of malocclusions—poor alignment—of teeth have made braces a rite of passage for many adolescents. No other mammals, even other primates, suffer from malocclusions to the extent that we do.

Part of the explanation for our shrinking jaws lies with genetic changes dating back to early human history. Those changes led to the remodeling of the skull and made room for a larger brain. Our jaws have also gotten smaller as a result of changes in our diet that have reduced the amount of muscular force we need to chew our food and the amount of time we must spend chewing it. Teeth have also gotten smaller over time, but not as rapidly as jaws, because tooth size is more strongly controlled by genetic factors and less influenced by diet.

For at least 300,000 years, humans have fragmented food with tools and used cooking to reduce its toughness. The advent of agriculture over 10,000 years ago increased humans' intake of cereals and other soft foods. More recently, improved techniques for milling grain and a host of other food-processing techniques have made it even easier to take in calories without exercising our jaws, a fact to which anyone who has gulped down a burger, fries, and shake can attest.

The result is a case of "use it or lose it." The fact that exerting muscular forces during chewing has an important effect on the jaws' development has been demonstrated experimentally. In one study, young pigs were fed a diet of soft food. After just a few months, their snouts were shorter and narrower and had thinner bones than pigs fed a diet of hard food.

"Magdalenian Girl," a 13,000- to 15,000-year-old skeleton found in southwestern France, had the earliest recorded case of impacted wisdom teeth. Anthropologists consider it evidence that dietary changes have long been a source of tooth troubles.

4

Bodily functions

Music of maturity

You can tell someone's approximate age by listening to his or her voice. I also think women's voices age more rapidly than men's, because I can more readily tell it is an older lady than an older man. What happens to the vocal cords as a person ages?

Shakespeare wrote about the aging individual, "turning again toward childish treble, pipes and whistles in his sound" (*As You Like It*, Act 2, Scene 7). Tests with modern acoustic equipment validate these poetic observations. Older people's voices can be distinguished by their characteristic decreases in loudness and clarity, changes in pitch, tremulousness, and breathiness.

The medical term for the normal age-related changes of the voice is presbylarynx. The prefix "presby" means elder. The larynx is the voice box. It lies in the middle of the neck and is composed of nine cartilages, held together by ligaments and controlled by muscles. Within the larynx are the vocal cords—paired ligaments covered by mucous membranes. Varying the length and tension of the ligaments produces sounds of different pitch.

All parts of the larynx have been observed to undergo age-related changes. Cartilage hardens, muscles atrophy, and nerves degenerate. The composition of the tissue in the vocal cords changes, which alters their mechanical properties. Dryness caused by diminished function of the mucus membranes in the larynx and decreased production of saliva affects the voice.

Respiratory health is also important, because air exhaled through the larynx creates the vibrations that produce sound. Therefore, the voice ages with decreases in the size and elasticity of the lungs, changes in the structure of the chest wall, and decreases in the force and rate of contraction of the muscles that control respiration.

Some physiological changes that age the voice differ by gender. In men, thinning of the outer layer of the vocal cords is common. As a result, the vocal cords may become bowed and fail to close completely, permitting air to escape through the gap and creating a wheezing sound. In women, the outer layer of the vocal cords tends to thicken, altering the vibration pattern and resulting in frequent breaks in pitch.

Changes in the thickness of the vocal cords are thought to be related to the testosterone/estrogen ratio, especially after menopause in women. Voice changes vary tremendously from person to person and appear to be more dependent on physiological age—overall health—than chronological age.

Prune people

What causes skin to wrinkle like a prune when a person is in a pool or bath?

The standard "stratum corneum" explanation is that we get wrinkly fingers and toes when water soaks into the outer layer of skin, the *stratum corneum* (Latin for "horny layer"). The stratum corneum is thickest on the palms and soles and consists of stacks of dead cells. When we dilly-dally in the tub, these dead cells absorb water and swell. The stratum corneum gets prune-like instead of puffy because it is firmly attached to the living skin beneath. Its surface area increases, but the surface area of the living skin stays the same. As a result, the stratum corneum buckles into a series of little ridges and valleys to accommodate its new surface area.

However, the observation that replanted fingers do not wrinkle after water immersion suggests that a different mechanism is responsible, or partly responsible, for wrinkling. A recent study found that blood flow to normal fingers decreased when people's hands were immersed in warm water, but in fingers that had been successfully reattached after accidental amputation, blood flow did not change. Wrinkling occurred and blood flow declined in the normal fingers of the same hand, and even the normal portion of the injured finger up to the reattachment point. Nerve damage in the reattached fingers may explain the blood flow response difference.

Based on these observations, the researchers suggested that constriction of blood vessels plays a key role in wrinkling. The digits contain large numbers of glomus organs—clusters of large, convoluted arteries that are involved in temperature regulation. The glomus organs are attached to the upper and lower layers of skin, so if they shrink, they would cause the overlying skin to be pulled inward. Uneven skin folds would then form because of the varying levels of tautness between the upper and lower layers of skin, at and amid the attachment points that anchor together the two layers.

The constriction of blood vessels in warm water is considered to be paradoxical. Usually it is a cold environment that causes a decrease in blood flow in the extremities to conserve body heat. When hands are heated with warm air, rather than warm water, blood flow increases.

The blood vessel constriction mechanism explains the difference in wrinkling between normal and replanted fingers. But it does not explain why blood vessel constriction in response to a cold environment does not lead to wrinkling. It may be that stratum corneum swelling and blood vessel constriction must occur together to cause fingers and toes to get all crinkly.

Blinky

Why do some people blink more than others?

One reason is that some people have dry eyes. Tear film, consisting of a layer of mucus, a layer of salty water, and a layer of oil, protects the outer surface of the eye. When the tear film thins or breaks up, nerve endings in the eye are exposed to environmental pollutants, including smoke, smog, and vapors from paint and cleaning products. Blinking helps alleviate the irritation by sweeping debris from the surface of the eye and stimulating the meibomian glands in the eyelid to release oil into the tear film.

Certain medications, such as allergy medicines, may cause dry eyes. Contact lenses interfere with the maintenance of a uniform tear film. Women are much more likely to suffer from dry eyes than men, in part because eye cosmetics can cause the tear film to break up. In addition, tear production declines with age, especially in women. The decline is probably related to decreased levels of estrogen and testosterone, which scientists postulate may help maintain the health of the glands that produce the tear film.

Destabilization of the tear film is not the only factor that affects blink rate. Typical blink frequencies at rest are about 12 to 20 blinks per minute. Studies have found that blink rate increases during conversation and when someone is anxious, but it can be suppressed during visual tasks that require concentration, such as reading.

Blink frequency is also affected in diseases, such as Parkinson's disease and Tourette's syndrome, which involve alterations in dopamine—a chemical that nerve cells use to communicate with each other—in the brain. These diseases may affect a "blink generator" in the brain thought to control involuntary blinking.

Blepharospasm is a condition that results in the forceful closing of one or both eyes. It appears to be a blink reflex gone awry.

Twitchy

Why does a human face occasionally twitch or have muscle spasms?

Twitching is a sudden, involuntary contraction and release of a muscle. Minor eyelid or facial spasms occur frequently and can be induced by stress, fatigue, eyestrain, caffeine, and certain medications. The exact mechanism that leads to these twitches is unknown, but normally muscle fibers are stimulated to contract by the release of calcium from little storage compartments within a muscle cell.

Hemifacial spasm is a more serious condition that results when an artery presses on the nerve to the facial muscles. Involuntary movements of the face can also result from disorders involving an area of the brain called the basal ganglia.

Summertime blues

If the human body runs at 98.6 degrees, why do we consider it hot when it's that warm outside?

To maintain a constant temperature, heat loss and heat production must be in balance. Our bodies produce heat as a byproduct of muscular activity and the chemical reactions of metabolizing food. Body heat radiates to the environment, but at a rate that decreases dramatically as the temperature of the environment increases.

When a part of the brain called the hypothalamus receives the message that the body is heating up, it sends out signals to make the blood vessels in the skin dilate. (This makes you feel more flushed but allows more heat to be released.) It also makes the sweat glands increase sweat output. Sweating cools you down because the evaporation of water uses heat.

If you have experienced the Midwest or East Coast during the three H's (hot, hazy, humid), you will appreciate how much more effective sweating is in a dry climate like San Diego!

Staying cool

Why do some people sweat more than others?

Age is one factor. The ability to sweat increases with maturation. Compared to sweat glands in adults, those in children are less sensitive to increases in body temperature and produce sweat more slowly. Sweating capacity is also lower in older adults relative to younger and middle-aged adults.

Gender plays a role. Women have a greater sweat gland density—number of sweat glands per unit area. Men produce more sweat per gland. Overall, women have a slightly lower sweat rate than men.

Heat acclimation has a large effect on the production of sweat and its composition. A person who is not acclimated to the heat usually cannot produce more than a quart (or liter) of sweat per hour. After someone has been exposed to hot weather for a few weeks, the sweat rate can double or triple. At the same time, the concentration of sodium chloride in the sweat declines to conserve body salt.

Hormones control the changes in sweating that result from heat exposure. Sweat comes from the fluid between cells, which is supplied by the blood vessels. Therefore, sweat is filtered blood plasma—the liquid (cell-free) portion of the blood. The sweating-related decrease in the water content of the blood leads to the production of antidiuretic hormone by the pituitary gland and to the production of aldosterone by the adrenal glands.

Antidiuretic hormone stimulates the kidneys to reabsorb water. Aldosterone stimulates the kidneys to reabsorb sodium. Repeated days of exercise in the heat can increase the volume of the blood plasma and the fluid between cells by 20 percent. Retention of water and salt prepares the body for subsequent sweat losses.

Aldosterone also stimulates the reabsorption of sodium and chloride by the cells that comprise the long, coiled tube of the sweat gland. However, potassium, calcium, magnesium, and other electrolytes found in sweat are not conserved, because the sweat gland does not have a mechanism to reabsorb them.

Sweating is initiated more quickly in physically fit people. More copious amounts of sweat are produced compared to less-fit people exercising at the same relative intensity (not engaging in the same task, but exerting themselves equally hard with respect to their own limitations).

Body size and composition can also play a role in sweating by limiting the body's ability to radiate heat to the environment so that more heat must be lost via evaporation. Other influences include hormonal imbalances and medications that stimulate the part of the nervous system that controls sweating.

Low thermostat

I have always sweated profusely. My normal body temperature is 96.8, and this is not a transposed figure. Is it possible that with my very low body temperature I suffer more in temperatures that others find chilly?

Average normal body temperature is 98.6 degrees Fahrenheit (37 degrees C), but temperatures as low as 95.9 degrees Fahrenheit (35.5 degrees C) and as high as 101.2 degrees Fahrenheit (38.4 degrees C) have been recorded in healthy people.

Maintenance of body temperature occurs through the balance of thermal energy generation from metabolizing food and the loss of thermal energy to the environment by conduction to other objects, convection due to air currents, radiation of infrared energy, and evaporation of sweat.

At rest, conduction, convection, and especially radiation account for most of the thermal energy transferred to the environment. The hotter a body is in relation to the environment, the more effective are these ways of getting rid of excess thermal energy. So someone with a naturally low body temperature must rely more on sweating to cool down.

Temperature is tightly regulated in humans, and relatively small increases in body temperature trigger sweating. On the other hand, camels can allow their body temperature to increase more than 10 degrees Fahrenheit (5.6 degrees C), which reduces the need for evaporative cooling through sweating and conserves water.

Sweaty gourmet

My daughter sweats when she eats, regardless of the temperature of the food or weather. I have never seen anyone else react the same. The sweat pours down her face.

Gustatory sweating—sweating in response to food—has various causes. Spicy food can stimulate the nerves that control the sweat glands. Also, thermal energy is generated as a byproduct of the digestion, absorption, and storage of food.

The amount of thermal energy generated in response to consuming an identical meal varies considerably among individuals. Gustatory sweating can also occur as a rare complication of diabetes.

Frey's syndrome is a special case of gustatory sweating that occurs when the nerve that controls the salivary gland is damaged by an accident or infection. The nerve's regrowth may be misdirected so that it connects with the nerve fibers that control the sweat glands. If this happens, any of the stimuli that would normally cause salivation—eating, the smell of food, or even the thought of food—can cause sweating on one or both sides of the face.

Impulsive impulses

When I observe my finger touching my toe, the touch feeling in finger and toe and the visual observation all occur simultaneously. How can the three nerve impulses (6 feet, 3 feet, and 4 inches) arrive at the brain simultaneously? I understand that nerve impulse speed is about 6 feet per second. This seems awfully slow, since I seem to feel the touch instantaneously.

If all nerve impulses traveled that slowly, you would be in trouble if you were a giraffe! Some nerve impulses do travel as slowly as 3 feet per second (about 1 meter per second), but others travel at speeds of over 200 feet per second (70 meters per second). Impulses travel more slowly along axons—long processes of the nerve cell—with smaller diameters.

The speed also depends on whether an axon is surrounded by myelin. Myelin consists of layers of membrane produced by special cells that envelop the nerve cells. Myelin acts as an electrical insulator and dramatically increases the speed at which the nerve impulse can travel. In diseases such as multiple sclerosis, in which myelin is destructively removed from the nerve, nerve impulses are slowed.

Myelin is rare in invertebrate organisms but is ubiquitous among vertebrates. Not all vertebrate axons are myelinated, but sensory nerves and nerves involved in movement are myelinated. Therefore, it takes only a fraction of a second for a nerve impulse to travel from the toe to the brain. As a result, the difference in impulse arrival times from the toe, finger, and eyes is too small for us to consciously distinguish.

American Lilliputians

How do our bodies know when to stop growing so that we do not become giants?

We would seem like giants to some populations of the past. A higher standard of living (better nutrition, less infectious disease) in many developed nations has led to significant increases in height with each generation. For example, in the past century, average height has increased about 4 inches in Japan and many European countries.

Intriguingly, Americans, who were the tallest in the world from colonial times to after World War II, have been surpassed by the Dutch, Swedes, Norwegians, Danes, British, and Germans, according to a study in *Economics and Human Biology* led by economist John Komlos. Komlos argues that universal access to health care and greater social equality in Northern Europe, relative to the United States, have led to healthier and taller populations.

Whatever the explanation, an immigration-related change in demographics does not seem to be it. When Komlos compared only non-Hispanic, non-Asian people who were born in the United States, Americans were still shorter than their Northern European counterparts.

Height is controlled by genetic programs that lead to the production of growth hormone and a cocktail of other hormones in our bodies. Exactly how environmental factors influence growth is not well understood, but scientists have a pretty good idea of the mechanisms through which hormones exert their influence on height.

Growth hormone is produced by the pituitary gland—a tiny organ near the base of the brain. In about 1 in 20,000 people, the pituitary gland produces too much growth hormone. If this happens in children before puberty, it can cause gigantism—excessive growth of the long bones in the limbs, as well as muscle and organ overgrowth.

Elongation of the bones in the arms and legs occurs at growth plates—regions near the ends of the bone consisting of cartilage. Stimulated by growth hormone, the cartilage cells reproduce, and the cartilage is later converted to compact bone. A variety of other hormones play a role in the proliferation and maturation of cartilage and the process by which it is removed and replaced with bone. Exercise also stimulates bone growth.

At puberty, the sex hormones (estrogen, testosterone) initially boost the release of growth hormone and lead to a growth spurt. Later, higher levels of sex hormones close the growth plates by causing the cartilage-producing cells to die and be replaced with bone.

Therefore, after puberty, an excess of growth hormone does not lead to gigantism. Instead, it can cause acromegaly—growth of soft features, resulting in enlarged feet, hands, and facial features.

Hair-raising

Why is it when you get scared the hairs on your arms and legs stand up?

Hair standing on end goes by many names: the pilomotor reflex, horripilation, cutis anserina, or, simply, goose bumps. It is part of the fight-or-flight reaction and is not unique to humans. You have probably seen a frightened feline assume a Halloween cat pose with fur puffed out, or a dog develop a bristling ruff when confronted by a rival.

Of course, humans are not particularly fuzzy mammals (with a few exceptions making an appearance on beaches and at poolside), and our pilomotor reflex does little to convince our enemies that we are bigger and should not be messed with. It may, in contrast, help us become consciously aware of our own fear response and make us more attentive to potential dangers in the environment.

Cold also causes our hair to stand on end. Again, this response works better for fuzzier mammals or birds. Lifting the hair or plumping feathers traps a layer of air close to the skin, which provides extra insulation.

Some people get goose bumps when listening to beautiful music or in other pleasurable situations. Stress and strong emotions (good or bad) activate the sympathetic nervous system, which prepares the body to respond to the stress. The sympathetic nervous system causes the contraction of a tiny muscle—the arrector pili (also called the erector pili)—that is attached to each hair follicle, the elongated pit that contains the hair. When the muscle contracts, it elevates the hair follicle to form a goose bump.

Puny puckers

How come we get goose bumps on our arms and legs, but not on our face?

Goose bumps can occur on the face. Facial hair follicles have arrector pili muscles that can elevate the follicle. But goose bumps do seem to be less obvious on the face.

The explanation is not the size of the hair or follicle, because a study found that average hair diameter and follicle diameter were similar on the face and on the body.

It may be because hair follicles are much more numerous on the face and head than on the rest of the body. Since the skin puckers at the site of the goose bump, the skin surrounding the goose bump must be pulled tighter. If the hair follicles are close together, as they are on the face, as the arrector pili contracts to lift the hair, the tightening of the skin between the hair follicles would oppose the lifting and result in flatter, less noticeable goose bumps. Facial skin is also thicker, and therefore more resistant to puckering, than skin on the forearms and calves, where goose bumps are very noticeable.

Earplugs

What are the source and purpose of earwax?

Earwax, or cerumen, is produced in the outer third of the ear, in the auditory canal. It is a mixture of secretions from the sebaceous or oil-producing glands and from modified apocrine or sweat glands. Cerumen lubricates the ear and prevents it from getting dry and itchy. It has antimicrobial properties and traps dust and debris.

Earwax also helps clean the ear because the skin in the auditory canal migrates out of the ear very slowly (about 1 millimeter every couple of weeks), carrying the wax that adheres to the skin, along with the dirt trapped in the wax.

Itchy and scratchy

When you have an itch on your back, and you or someone else scratches it, why does the itchy spot seem to move from one spot to another? Sometimes scratching makes your entire back itchy. Why?

Detection and alleviation of itchiness involve nerve pathways for itch, tickle, and pain. The pathways are distinct, but each involves receptors in the skin to detect the sensation, nerves to relay the information to the brain, and nerves to relay information from the brain back to the skin.

Scratching reduces itchiness by removing whatever is causing the itch, such as a hair or an insect. If the cause of the itch cannot be removed—for example, because the skin has launched an allergic reaction to the saliva in a mosquito bite—we may find ourselves scratching until it hurts. The pain signal occupies the central nervous system so that it "forgets" about the itch signal, at least temporarily. The sting of rubbing alcohol also helps soothe the itch of an insect bite for this reason.

When someone else scratches you, the receptors for tickle can be activated. When we touch our own bodies, inhibitory signals from the brain suppress the tickle response. Inhibitory signals from the brain also kick in to shut down the itch response when a large area of the skin is scratched or rubbed, so it may feel like you need to scratch your entire back to make the itch go away.

Scratching can sometimes make the situation worse, because scratching may cause mast cells in the skin to release histamine, which causes inflammation and itchiness. Scratching is more likely to stimulate the release of histamine if someone is already experiencing an allergic reaction or has very dry skin.

Heart-stopping

Does your heart stop when you sneeze?

No. The heart's rhythm is controlled by a natural pacemaker—the sinoatrial node, a group of cells located in the right atrium of the heart. These cells create an electrical impulse by pumping charged particles out of the cell and then allowing them to flow back in. Conducting cells transmit the electrical impulse to all parts of the heart to initiate muscle contraction. Sneezing does not stop this electrical activity.

On the other hand, the nervous system and circulating hormones, such as adrenalin, alter the rate of the electrical activity in the sinoatrial node to increase or decrease heart rate. Just as exercise increases the heart rate, sneezing works many muscles; therefore, it is possible for a "sneeze attack" to increase the heart rate.

Sneeze grimace

Why can't you sneeze with your eyes open?

A close relationship exists between the protective reflexes of the nose and eyes. When something like pollen irritates the mucous membranes in the nose, the trigeminal nerve is stimulated, and it relays the message to a sneeze integration center in the medulla at the base of the brain.

The sneeze center is mission control for the sneeze reflex, and it coordinates three simultaneous actions. It commands the respiratory muscles to produce an explosive inspiration and then expiration. It causes the glands in the nose to produce mucous, and it triggers facial muscles to close the eyes and grimace.

Photon allergy

Why do I always sneeze when I step into bright sunlight?

You have a photic sneeze reflex, also known as ACHOO Syndrome. If you want to impress your friends, ACHOO stands for autosomal dominant compelling helio-ophthalmic outburst. (I'm not sure why it's not ADCHOO, but at least sneeze scientists have a sense of humor.)

About one-quarter of the population has this reflex, and it is thought to be genetic. The reflex varies in strength, with some people affected only in bright sunlight and others affected by camera flashes or other light sources.

The number of sneezes initiated in bright light varies among individuals. And some people even have a sneeze reflex when they rub the corner of their eye, pluck their eyebrows, or comb their hair.

Scientists are not exactly sure what causes ACHOO Syndrome. It is known that the sneezing integration center at the base of the brain receives neural inputs from other parts of the brain as well as the nose.

In photic sneezers, bright light may directly or indirectly stimulate nerves that usually respond when something irritates your nose. This information gets sent to the sneezing integration center, which in turn sends signals to coordinate the diverse muscle groups needed for the sneeze.

Sleeping beauty

What goes on in your body while you are sleeping?

Until the late 1950s, the dominant view was that sleep was simply an idling state. However, electroencephalograms (EEGs), which record fluctuations of electrical activity in groups of nerve cells in the brain, have shown that the sleeping brain is active and that sleep is composed of identifiable stages that occur in cycles throughout the night.

About 30 to 45 minutes after falling asleep, a person enters slow-wave sleep, which is characterized by slow-frequency brain waves. As a sleeper progresses through stages 1 to 4 of slow-wave sleep, the EEG records brain waves that are progressively slower frequency and higher voltage.

The muscles are relaxed during slow-wave sleep, but the sleeper shifts posture regularly. Heart rate and blood pressure decrease. Stage-4 sleep is the deepest and most difficult to interrupt. Someone awakened from stage-4 sleep feels groggy and confused.

By about 90 minutes after the initiation of sleep, the sleeper has progressed back through stages 4 to 1 of slow-wave sleep, and the EEG pattern changes abruptly. The EEG records low-voltage, high-frequency brain waves, similar to those observed in the waking state. This is rapid eye movement or REM sleep, and if awakened, most sleepers will recall dreaming. Sleepers awakened from slow-wave sleep may recall an image or emotion, but rarely a story-like dream.

The pons—an area at the base of the brain—keeps the body in a state of paralysis throughout REM sleep, although the muscles controlling eye movements and respiration are not inhibited. During REM sleep, the body even ceases to regulate its temperature.

Cats with damage to the pons appear to act out their dreams, such as stalking and pouncing as if they were chasing mice. People can also have "REM behavior disorder." One sleeper, who had been dreaming he was a football player charging an opponent, woke up with a gash on his head from tackling his dresser.

Depriving people of sleep right after they are trained to do a task interferes with learning, even when people are tested a week later, after recouping their sleep. Brain-imaging studies with animals reveal that the pattern of brain activity that occurs during the learning of a task, such as navigating a maze, is replayed during sleep. Greater replay during sleep translates into greater learning.

The exact mechanisms through which sleep facilitates learning and memory are not understood. However, certain genes known to play a role in changing connections between nerve cells are switched on in the brain during post-training sleep.

Yawning maw

I have often wondered what triggers a yawn.

According to folk belief, we yawn because we are not breathing in enough oxygen. The deep inhalation that is a major feature of the yawn makes this idea appealing, but compelling evidence exists that this explanation is not entirely correct.

When people were made to breathe air with higher-than-normal levels of carbon dioxide, their respiration rate increased, but they did not yawn more than people breathing normal air. The number of yawns also did not change when people breathed pure oxygen. Therefore, respiration rate, rather than yawning, seems to regulate oxygen intake.

So why do we yawn? One possibility is that yawning stimulates us to stay awake. In support of this hypothesis, studies have shown that people yawn frequently in the hour before they go to bed but rarely yawn when they are trying to fall asleep. People also yawn frequently while driving. Zoo and laboratory animals yawn before their normal feeding time. Yawning seems to occur when it is important to stay awake.

How would yawning help us stay awake? Some scientists think yawning may dilate the arteries that bring blood to the brain, thereby increasing cerebral blood flow.

The exact trigger for the yawn remains elusive. Certain research suggests that an oxygen sensor, located in a part of the brain known as the hypothalamus, initiates the yawn in response to low levels of oxygen in the brain. Since blood carries oxygen, this research is consistent with the idea that yawning causes a jump in blood flow to the brain, but it does not explain why breathing air containing less oxygen does not induce yawning.

Many different brain chemicals can induce or inhibit yawning, but because the effects of these chemicals are often studied by injecting them into the brains of anesthetized animals, it is unclear which play a role under normal conditions.

An enigmatic feature of yawning is that it appears to be contagious. Perhaps you have yawned while reading this answer. Seeing someone yawn, and reading about and thinking about yawning, can cause humans to yawn.

Although nearly all vertebrates (even fish, frogs, and birds) yawn, until recently humans were the only species known to yawn contagiously. However, recent research has shown that chimps yawned more when watching a video of other chimps yawning. Images of grinning chimps did not have the same effect. Not all the chimps were susceptible to contagious yawning, but neither are all humans.

The fact that yawning is contagious has led researchers to suggest that it may have evolved as a way of synchronizing the social behavior of groups. College lecture halls are a good place to observe vestiges of this evolutionary mechanism.

Smells good

Everything in our world has a scent. Has anyone ever been able to identify how many scents and odors exist in our world?

If we humans were to count all the scents in the world, we would come up with a different number than the other members of the animal kingdom. Dogs, for instance, can detect odors at concentrations almost 100 million times lower than humans can.

There is also much variation among humans in how well we can smell: Some people are unable to perceive certain smells, women generally have a more sensitive sense of smell than men, and as we age we lose our ability to discriminate between smells.

You get a whiff of something because small, volatile molecules from that thing have become airborne, and you have breathed them in. New paint smells because molecules in the paint are evaporating and dissolving in the mucus that lines your nasal passages. When all the volatile molecules have evaporated, paint loses its smell.

At the top of your nasal passages are two postage stamp-sized patches of cells that contain olfactory, or scent, receptors. Estimates of the number of olfactory receptor cells vary widely. Humans likely have somewhere in the range of 10 million of these cells, while scent-tracking bloodhounds have about a billion.

Your brain finds out about a smell when molecules bind to the olfactory receptors in your nose. Scent molecules activate different receptors, with each type of receptor thought to respond to no more than a handful of different smells. The pattern of activation of olfactory receptors seems to work something like a bar code from which the brain determines the smell's identity.

Some controversy exists among scientists about just how olfactory receptors become activated, but currently the most compelling explanation is that smell molecules activate receptors into which they fit, like a key in a lock.

Of the five senses, smell remains the most difficult for scientists to explain. Coffee, bacon, and cigarette smoke all have hundreds of volatile molecules, yet we do not detect the individual components. But we can detect the distinct fragrances of coffee, bacon, and cigarette smoke when all three are mixed together.

Previously scientists estimated that we should be able to distinguish 10,000 different smells. However, from our current understanding of smell discrimination, in theory we should be able to distinguish an almost infinite number of smells.

One of the most enigmatic features of smell is how the mere hint of an aroma can conjure up powerful memories. For example, the smell of apple pie might take you back to your grandmother's kitchen. This is because information about smell is sent to the hippocampus, a part of the brain concerned with emotion, motivation, and certain kinds of memory.

Tip of the tongue

Please explain this apparently common phenomenon. You are trying to remember the name of someone you knew a long time ago. Despite earnest and repeated attempts to recall the name, it eludes you. When you are no longer trying to think of it, the name suddenly pops into your brain.

The very mechanisms that help us concentrate can cause thoughts to shy away from us like skittish horses, only to return when we have stopped pursuing them.

To make knowledge more accessible, our brains suppress conceptual distractions through a process known as retrieval-induced forgetting. Researchers have most commonly studied this active process of forgetting using word retrieval tests.

For instance, people learn lists of category–exemplar pairs (fruits–apple, fruits–plum, fruits–banana) for several categories (fruits, sports, cars, dog breeds). They then practice retrieving some of the exemplars when cued with the category and the first two letters of the exemplar (fruits–pl__). Later, they are given the categories and asked to recall all the exemplars from each category.

As expected, retrieval practice improves recall of the reviewed material. Surprisingly, recall of the category–exemplar pairs that were not practiced is worse than it is when people do not practice retrieving any of the category–exemplar pairs at all. In other words, the recall of one memory causes the suppression of related memories.

Brain imaging has shown that retrieval-induced forgetting is adaptive because it reduces the demands on the cognitive control mechanisms needed to recall one of the competing memories.

Unfortunately, it also trips us up when we are searching for that less-used memory. It has even been shown to be responsible for what can seem like deliberate lapses of native-language words in novices after immersion in a foreign language.

Retrieval-induced forgetting shuts off when we are no longer trying to actively recall a memory. The thread of a related memory can then lead us to the forgotten memory. Memories are more like spiderwebs than file folders, because different aspects of a memory (such as someone's name or image or an event involving the individual) are stored in different parts of the brain.

Mood also affects forgetting and recall. Studies have shown that positive moods enhance retrieval-induced forgetting, and negative moods inhibit it. This is because positive moods encourage global processing of information and connections between related ideas (connections that can lead to suppression of a memory during active attempts at retrieval), whereas negative moods encourage item-specific processing. Later though, when one is no longer trying to recall something and it is no longer being actively suppressed, a positive mood can enhance retrieval by making it more likely that a connection will be forged to the elusive memory.

A particularly intriguing insight into recall comes from people with synesthesia—a mixing of the senses. In one form of synesthesia, lexical-gustatory synesthesia, hearing, seeing, saying, or thinking about a word leads to specific, detailed food experiences, as well as activation of the brain region responsible for the perception of taste. For example, for one lexical-gustatory synesthete, the word "part" tasted like chicken noodle soup. When they have a word on the tip of their tongues, lexical-gustatory synesthetes can taste the word before they can retrieve it. This is consistent with the notion that memories have many components and connections, and access to an individual component can be blocked without affecting other connections.

5

Pesky pathogens

Bundle up

Do you get a cold from being cold? I sat in an unheated library yesterday, and today my nose is streaming.

Modern virology textbooks reject the idea that being cold makes one catch a cold. The standard explanation of why colds are more prevalent in the winter than in the summer is that people spend more time indoors in contact with each other in the winter, which facilitates the spread of the viruses that cause colds.

Still, the folklore surrounding the relationship between cold exposure and the common cold is so longstanding and widespread that a number of researchers have considered it worthy of further exploration. Their studies suggest that Mom's advice to "Keep warm so that you don't catch a cold" may not have been off the mark after all.

One study of populations in seven countries in Europe, from Finland to Greece, showed that there were fewer deaths from respiratory diseases in regions where people tended to take protective measures against the cold. These included heating their homes, wearing protective clothes, and being physically active, rather than standing and shivering, when outdoors.

In the study, a given fall in temperature claimed more lives in regions with mild winters, and people in these regions were less likely to bundle up and heat their homes. For example, at the same outdoor temperature, 45 degrees Fahrenheit (7 degrees C), only 13 percent of people in Athens wore hats, whereas 72 percent of people in south Finland wore them. In addition, average living room temperatures were 4 degrees Fahrenheit (2.2 degrees C) warmer in southern Finland than in Athens.

Experimental studies on the effect of cold exposure have been mixed. One hypothesis to explain this inconsistency is that getting chilled makes a difference if a person not only has been exposed to one of the more than 200 cold viruses but also is already in the process of fighting the infection. In other words, cold exposure can turn an asymptomatic infection into full-fledged, nose-tooting misery.

Being cold may lead to the release of stress hormones, which suppress the body's immune system. Low temperatures also cause the blood vessels in the nose and upper airways to constrict, possibly reducing the access of blood cells responsible for attacking invaders. In addition, cold air damps the action of cilia—tiny moving hairs that help eliminate contaminants in the airways.

So while doctors' advice to wash your hands and avoid sick people will help you stay healthy, taking precautions against getting chilled may also help you fight the good fight against those insidious germs.

Invader individuality

During cold season, we are told that antibiotics will not kill viruses and that colds are caused by a virus. What is the difference between viruses and bacteria, and why is it so hard to come up with a medicine to kill viruses?

Bacteria are single-celled organisms that contain the machinery needed to grow and replicate. Antibiotics inhibit various life processes in bacteria. Penicillin and related compounds interfere with the systems that build the cell walls of bacteria. Tetracyclines, as well as erythromycin and its relatives, block the bacterial cell's machinery for making new proteins. Other antibiotics prevent bacteria from duplicating DNA, or from using or making essential nutrients.

Viruses are smaller than bacteria and basically consist of genetic material (RNA or DNA) packaged in a protein shell. Viruses cannot provide their own energy or replicate on their own. To reproduce, viruses must hijack the cellular machinery of another organism. Since antibiotics and antivirals must target processes that are unique to the infectious agents to avoid harming the cells of the infected organism, the simplicity of viruses means that they have fewer Achilles' heels than bacteria. Also, viruses can hide within cells, in some cases for many years.

Thirty years ago, just three antiviral drugs were available. Genome sequencing and the study of the replication cycle of viruses have since led to major advances because antiviral drugs must be tailored to the viruses they attack. Knowledge of the structures and functions of the viral enzymes, or catalysts, guides the design of drugs that specifically block those enzymes. A similar procedure is used to develop antibiotics, although some—broad-spectrum antibiotics—are effective against a range of bacteria.

More than 40 drugs for the treatment of viral infections have now been approved, about half of which are used to treat HIV infections. One example of an antiviral medication is AZT, which inhibits an enzyme used by HIV to copy its genes into the genetic material of the cells it infects. Other antiviral medications prevent viruses from getting into cells, and still others prevent the finished virus particles from leaving cells and spreading elsewhere in the body.

Viruses and bacteria both mutate and become resistant to the drugs designed to fight them. Like the Red Queen in the sequel to *Alice's Adventures in Wonderland*—running as fast as possible just to stay in place—researchers must continually develop new strategies to overcome drug resistance.

Moving target

Influenza viruses are known to mutate into new, sometimes more virulent forms, which explains why some of us periodically get sick. Why is it that the same is not true for other known viruses, such as the polio and smallpox viruses?

Influenza viruses do evolve particularly quickly. Vaccine strains used against influenza must be changed at least every two to three years, because the proteins on the virus surface keep changing, thereby disguising it from the immune system. Vaccines against polio and many other human viruses have been stable for decades.

Part of what determines how fast a virus mutates is the type of genetic material it uses. Some viruses have genomes consisting of DNA. A chemically similar molecule, RNA, serves as the genetic material for other viruses. Another type of virus, the retrovirus, has RNA as its genetic material but copies RNA into DNA within an infected cell.

As a general rule, DNA viruses mutate more slowly than retroviruses, which mutate more slowly than RNA viruses. The fastest-mutating RNA virus has a mutation rate about 100,000 times faster than the slowest-mutating DNA virus. This range reflects the accuracy and proofreading ability of the machinery used to copy the different types of genetic material.

The genome of the variola (smallpox) virus is DNA, and a comparison of 45 virus samples from around the world during the 30 years prior to the eradication of smallpox revealed little sequence diversity. Yet genetic spellchecking is not the whole story, because polio, measles, and influenza are all caused by RNA viruses.

The mutation rate in viruses is also influenced by their generation time, genomic architecture (how the DNA or RNA is folded and whether it is single- or double-stranded), viral and host enzymes, and opportunities for virus particles to exchange genetic material with one another.

Yet higher mutation rates do not always enhance evolution. In an experiment in which the mutation rate of poliovirus was artificially increased by a factor of 10, the production of the virus decreased 1,000-fold, probably the result of an error catastrophe. In fact, increasing mutation rates to a lethal level is the mechanism of some antiviral drugs, such as ribavirin, a treatment for hepatitis C.

Therefore, mutation rate is insufficient to explain why influenza is a master of disguise compared to other RNA viruses, and the specific constraint on the evolution of surface protein variation remains a mystery.

Bug buddies

Are any viruses nonpathogenic and used by our bodies, much like a lot of bacteria help us digest our food and so on?

"Bacteria are our friends" claims an adorably nerdy T-shirt sported by some biologists. Those who would roll their eyes at what they view to be a fashion faux pas have undoubtedly at least heard of beneficial bacteria. Ongoing research shows that our microscopic buddies do even more for us than we once thought. Related research suggests that viruses may also merit their own fan club.

About 1,000 species of normal, or commensal, bacteria inhabit our bodies. In total, we are lugging around a few pounds of bacteria. These bacterial cells, which are smaller than our own cells, significantly outnumber the human cells in our bodies. The highest concentration of bacteria is found in our intestines, especially the colon, and bacteria comprise approximately 60 percent of the solids in feces.

Commensal bacteria synthesize important nutrients and digest various compounds. Laboratory animals raised under sterile conditions retain water in their intestines because they lack bacteria that break down mucus. These animals also have altered immune systems.

Commensal bacteria stimulate the developing immune system but also help it develop regulatory mechanisms that prevent it from overreacting and causing chronic inflammation. Furthermore, they provide a physical barrier against disease-causing organisms, which may invade after treatment with antibiotics inadvertently wipes out our bacterial friends.

Viruses must hijack the machinery in a host organism's cells to replicate. The hijacked cell may be killed, or at least prevented from carrying out its normal function. This is not a very happy state of affairs, unless the cells the virus infects are themselves dangerous invaders. This is the case with some bacteriophages (phages)—tiny viruses that infect bacteria.

Recent evidence suggests that phage predation on the bacteria that cause cholera—a waterborne diarrhea disease—can explain why most cholera epidemics tend to be self-limiting. A study found that as the cholera bacteria spread, the phages that prey on them became more abundant in the environment and in stool samples of those infected with cholera, until the epidemic rapidly collapsed.

Phage therapy has also been used successfully to treat diseases. Some researchers have hypothesized that phages play a normal role in regulating the ecosystem of bacteria in our bodies, and that they may contribute to our immune defenses to other viruses and even cancer.

Maybe T-shirts saying "Viruses are our friends" are about to come into vogue. If they do, you read it here first.

Laid low

Why do we ache when we get sick with a cold or the flu?

The warfare used by our bodies against an invading virus, rather than damage from the virus itself, causes symptoms of the common cold and the flu. In response to infection, white blood cells release chemicals to communicate with other cells. These chemical messages amplify the triggering event (detection of a virus) and activate whole-body defense responses.

One chemical that plays a dominant role is bradykinin, which is a peptide, or small protein. It causes aches by stimulating sensory nerves. Other chemicals, including histamine and prostaglandins, may sensitize nerve endings to bradykinin. Bradykinin also causes other symptoms. When administered into the noses of healthy volunteers, it causes a runny, congested nose and throat irritation.

These symptoms make us feel miserable, but they ultimately help us get well. For example, fever facilitates the destruction of viruses and bacteria. Even cold-blooded lizards move to warmer places when they have an infection, and if prevented from warming their bodies above their usual temperature, they are more likely to die from the infection.

Similarly, that annoying stuffy nose may inhibit virus replication by raising the temperature of the nasal passages. Viruses that cause upper-airway infections generally propagate best at temperatures a few degrees below body temperature—conditions found in nasal passages cooled by inhaled air, but not in a congested airway.

Aches and fatigue also serve an adaptive purpose by making us rest, thereby directing more of our resources toward fighting infection (and making us feel less guilty about curling up in bed with a cup of cocoa and a good book).

Fever favor

You stated previously, "Fever facilitates the destruction of viruses and bacteria." Then why do we take medication to lower the body's temperature when we have a fever? Once our body temperature has been lowered (from the meds), is our body still fighting the invaders?

Most cold and flu medications are designed to relieve the symptoms of the illness so that we can function better, but they do not cure the viral infection. Fever-reducing drugs—collectively known as antipyretics—seem to be effective at reducing the mental dysfunction sometimes observed in patients with fever. Most antipyretics are also analgesics, or painkillers.

Fever increases metabolic demands and may stress a patient. Fever has also been associated with seizures in children. However, despite the widespread use of antipyretics, these drugs have failed to prevent fever-associated seizures in experimental studies.

Our bodies are still fighting the infection when we take antipyretics, but some studies have shown that taking antipyretics may slightly worsen symptoms or prolong illness. For example, patients infected with rhinovirus (which causes the common cold) who were treated with aspirin or acetaminophen had worse nasal congestion and produced virus particles longer than patients who were not treated with antipyretics.

Healthy as a dog

My dog never gets ill, yet everyone in my house gets colds, flu, etc. From what I have witnessed, humans seem to be the most disease-prone of any species on the planet. What is the reason for this?

Your dog is probably healthier because he is exposed to fewer other dogs than humans are exposed to other humans. Humans and dogs are susceptible to many of the same types of diseases, including parasitic, viral, and bacterial infections. Canine infectious respiratory disease, or "kennel cough," is a significant problem in boarding facilities and other densely housed dog populations.

Infectious disease is also a problem in livestock, especially animals raised in crowded conditions. Just as history is full of examples of human populations that succumbed to diseases carried by explorers and colonists, domestic and wild-animal populations also have suffered after exposure to foreign germs.

Children in daycare have a higher incidence of colds than children without extensive contact with other children outside the home. We develop immunity as we get older; preschoolers have about six to ten colds per year compared to two to four in adults. However, immunity usually protects only against repeat infections with the same virus, and at least 200 known viruses cause colds.

Keep off the grass

I am concerned about bodily fluids released onto the increasingly popular synthetic playing fields during practices and sporting events. What are schools/colleges/stadiums doing to minimize the growth of potentially dangerous bacteria within the 3-D realm of the turf material?

Bacteria and viruses last a disturbingly long time on various types of surfaces. Studies of disease-causing bacteria and viruses have shown that many species survive days, weeks, months, or even years. Most survive longest under cool, humid conditions.

Synthetic turf has gotten a bad rap from reports that athletes who train mostly on synthetic fields may be at a greater risk of skin infections than athletes who train on grass fields. For example, during one season, five of 58 players on the St. Louis Rams football team got methicillin-resistant *Staphylococcus aureus* (MRSA) skin infections. Some opposing players developed MRSA infections after playing the Rams on their artificial turf.

Scientists from the Centers for Disease Control and Prevention (CDC) investigated the outbreak of MRSA among Rams players and opponents but did not find any MRSA on the artificial turf. Of course, this is like searching for a needle in a haystack, so it does not prove that the bacteria are absent. But the general consensus is that the turf is not the most likely source of the bacteria that caused the outbreak.

Instead, the CDC concluded that artificial turf can increase athletes' susceptibility to skin infections because falls on artificial turf often lead to "turf burns." Turf burns are especially common on older-model fields like the one the Rams played on, which lack a cushioning rubber/sand base. The raw skin of a turf burn provides an easy entry point for bacteria.

The athletes themselves are the most likely source of the bacteria, which spread through skin-to-skin contact. Close to one-third of people carry *Staphylococcus aureus* on their skin or in their noses, and about 1 percent of people carry the MRSA strain that resists the class of antibiotics that has traditionally been used to treat *Staphylococcus aureus* infections. MRSA was mostly unknown outside the hospital setting until the late 1990s, but it has become increasingly common in the community since then.

Antibacterial sprays can be applied to artificial turf, but no research has been conducted on their effectiveness in preventing disease. To prevent skin infections, the CDC recommends showering after working out, keeping wounds covered, and avoiding the sharing of personal items such as towels and razors.

Vexing virus

Why is it so difficult to find a cure for AIDS?

Drug and vaccine development is complicated because HIV—the immunodeficiency virus that causes AIDS—is a "moving target." HIV mutates frequently, resulting in different genetic variants of HIV being prevalent in different populations and even multiple variants within an infected individual.

The first HIV drug was introduced in 1987 with much excitement, but HIV resistance soon arose. Now more than 20 HIV drugs have been approved by the U.S. Food and Drug Administration. An increased understanding of HIV has made it possible to design drugs that interfere with different stages of the virus's life cycle.

HIV multiplies in certain cells of the immune system, destroying them in the process. The virus recognizes a cell, binds to it, fuses with it, and injects its genetic material into the cell. HIV is a retrovirus—its genetic material is RNA, from which the virus's reverse transcriptase enzyme produces DNA. Viral DNA is then integrated into the host cell's DNA. This enables HIV to exploit the cell's machinery to make more viral RNA and viral proteins, which are packaged into new virus particles.

Current HIV treatments usually combine multiple drugs. For example, one or more drugs that block reverse transcriptase may be combined with a protease inhibitor—a drug that interferes with the processing steps necessary to make mature viral proteins. Since these drugs work in different ways, the virus would need to develop multiple mutations to resist all of them.

Determining the genetic makeup of the HIV infecting a patient has also become a part of standard care. The information is used to help predict what drugs are likely to be effective against the variants of HIV that infect the patient, and what drugs are likely to fail because of resistance. When necessary, treatment regimens can be altered to keep up with an evolving virus.

HIV drugs can have serious side effects, and patients have difficulty staying on complicated regimens, requiring them to take multiple pills each day. In addition, HIV can lie dormant in cells for many years, making it difficult to completely eradicate. Still, in the developed world, these therapies have led to a drastic improvement in the prognosis for HIV-infected patients.

Sadly, progress has been much slower in the developing world. Cost is one complication. Treatment of one HIV patient in the Unites States runs approximately $20,000 per year. Another is that patients often lack access to medical experts who can monitor and respond to drug resistance and side effects.

Cure claims

I have heard that there is a way to treat hepatitis C infections that is more effective than the conventional treatment. What is this cure called, and what does it consist of?

The World Health Organization estimates that approximately 3 percent of the world population has been infected with the hepatitis C virus (HCV), which can be transmitted by sharing needles, sexually, and through blood transfusions received before donors were screened for HCV (1992 in the United States). In about one-quarter of cases, the infection clears up on its own. Of those who remain chronically infected, a subset will develop cirrhosis of the liver. HCV infection is the most frequent reason for liver transplantation.

Current treatment for chronic HCV infection is a combination of ribavirin and interferon, usually administered for several months. These medicines are effective for just over half of patients. They are more effective with some strains of HCV than others. The treatment also has a number of side effects and is unsuitable for patients with certain health conditions.

Other treatments are under development, including small molecules designed to block different steps in the viral replication process. Unfortunately, the virus quickly evolves resistance to these drugs, but drug cocktails that contain a variety of replication blockers may ultimately prove effective.

A plethora of alternative treatments for HCV are being promoted. Surveys of HCV patients in the United States reveal that about 40 percent of them take alternative medicines for HCV, mostly herbal products, often in addition to conventional treatment.

Because these herbal preparations have not been rigorously tested and are not regulated by the Food and Drug Administration, conventional medical professionals are concerned about their safety and value. In a review of the management of HCV published in 2006 in the journal *Gastroenterology*, the American Gastroenterological Association concluded that alternative therapies do not have a role in the treatment of hepatitis C.

Other researchers (see reviews of alternative treatments for HCV infections in *Antiviral Therapy*, volume 12, page 285, and *Journal of Hepatology*, volume 40, page 491) are less dismissive and call for large-scale, properly designed clinical trials on these herbal products to help people make informed decisions about them. The National Institutes of Health recently began a clinical trial on the most popular herbal treatment for HCV, *Silybum marianum*—milk thistle. Glycyrrhizin—an extract of licorice root—and extracts of bovine thymic gland have shown mildly promising results. To learn more about HCV clinical trials, visit http://www.clinicaltrials.gov.

Food zapper

With the demise of SureBeam, are there any other players left for the possible irradiation of incoming products from Mexico or other countries? Many of us thought that irradiation would provide protection against coliforms and salmonella, which frequently occur on produce and other foodstuffs.

The now-bankrupt company SureBeam produced electron beam food irradiation systems. Two alternative methods exist for the irradiation of food: gamma rays and X-rays. Gamma rays are produced by radioactive cobalt. X-rays and electron beams are generated electrically, which allows them to be switched on and off. Despite this advantage, irradiation with gamma rays is generally the preferred method because X-rays are more expensive to produce, and electron beams do not penetrate deeply into food.

At low doses, irradiation kills insects, delays fruit ripening, and prevents vegetables from sprouting. At medium doses, it reduces disease-causing microbes as well as bacteria, molds, and yeast that cause food spoilage. Hospitals use irradiation at higher doses to sterilize meals for patients who have weak immune systems. NASA has also used irradiation at high doses to sterilize meat for astronauts. Irradiation works by damaging DNA, which interferes with cellular processes and cell division.

In 1963 the U.S. Food and Drug Administration first approved irradiation to rid wheat, wheat flour, and potatoes of insects. Since the mid-1980s the FDA has approved irradiation of spices, meat, and fresh fruit and vegetables. Currently only 10 percent of herbs and spices and less than 1 percent of meat and produce are irradiated in the United States.

Opposition, rather than lack of technology, has slowed the implementation of irradiation. One set of arguments concerns the safety and nutritional quality of irradiated food. Like any method of food preservation and preparation, irradiation results in small losses of nutrients. Irradiation also results in the formation of 2-alkylcyclobutanones—chemicals that are unique to irradiated foods. The World Health Organization and other public health agencies have reviewed the scientific studies and concluded that irradiated foods are safe.

Others oppose additional processing of food and express concern that irradiation makes it possible to cover up unsanitary food handling, especially fecal contamination. Avoiding fecal contamination is critical for preventing food-borne viral diseases because the small size of viruses makes them resistant to irradiation at doses approved for foods. Bacterial spores—the dense, hardy, hibernation state of bacteria—are also resistant to irradiation. Therefore, irradiation can be an additional food safety tool, not a cure-all.

Laboratory life

I read that it took three years to create in 2002 the first virus made from scratch with commercially available ingredients. Does this mean that we can "create life" now?

A paper published in the journal *Science* in August 2002 describes the creation of poliovirus from scratch based on its genetic blueprint. The researchers first synthesized a string of approximately 7,500 nucleotides (the chemical building blocks of RNA and DNA) according to the known genetic sequence of poliovirus. They then added the virus's synthesized genome to a solution containing enzymes (catalysts) and amino acids (building blocks of protein). This step permitted the appropriate virus proteins to be synthesized.

To prove that the newly created virus worked, the researchers injected it into mice. As expected for the virus that causes polio, the mice became paralyzed.

About a year later, another group synthesized a virus in just two weeks, surprisingly fast compared to the three years it took to make the first virus from scratch. Still, both viruses have relatively small genomes compared to other viruses. Synthesizing a genome gets more complex as the number of nucleotides that need to be linked increases.

Whether or not we can now create life depends on your definition of life, a topic that has given rise to much philosophical pondering. Some scientists do not consider a virus to be "alive" because viruses cannot reproduce on their own. They exploit the machinery of the cell they infect to make it churn out new virus particles. Other scientists consider viruses to be alive because they contain sufficient genetic information for self-existence.

On the other hand, bacteria are certainly alive, but no one has made bacteria from scratch yet. Building bacteria has two major complications. First, bacteria have larger genomes than viruses. Second, while the simplest viruses consist of a string of nucleotides surrounded by a few proteins, bacteria are cells with complicated component parts that have specialized functions. So human-created bacteria remain in the realm of science fiction for now.

Building organisms

Why are scientists unable to create life?

Swapping genes between species has been possible for over 30 years, but building a living cell remains a holy grail for biologists. By assembling a cell from small molecules, they would gain valuable knowledge of cellular function, just as engineers gain a better understanding of how a machine works by constructing it than by merely studying it.

Biologists have synthesized small viruses, but viruses are basically strands of genetic material—RNA or DNA—packaged with a few proteins. Many scientists do not consider them alive because they must exploit the cellular machinery of a host organism to reproduce.

On the other hand, even the simplest bacterial cell has complex component parts that allow it to take in food, eliminate waste, replicate genetic material, build proteins, and repair and expand the cell membrane. Building all of these parts from scratch is technically challenging.

Progress is being made. It is now possible to build cell-like compartments that can produce protein. A published blueprint details the genes and component parts predicted to be sufficient to assemble a minimal cell that can survive under controlled laboratory conditions. Also, recent research has shown that it is possible to remove and replace the entire genome of a bacterial cell.

Efforts are under way to synthesize a minimal genome and place it in a bacterial cell that has had its own genetic material removed. The result would not be a completely synthetic organism. Still, it would be an intermediate step that would reveal whether researchers have identified all the genes necessary for life. Many researchers are optimistic that a fully synthetic cell is not far off.

Tick bites

I was bitten by a tick at the base of Palomar Mountain near San Diego. The tick was on me for about one to two hours. I never got a rash. Is Lyme disease present in that area?

Lyme disease is spread via the bite of a tick infected with *Borrelia burgdorferi* bacteria. The first symptom, experienced by about 80 percent of those infected with Lyme disease, is a red rash around and expanding out from the bite. The rash generally occurs within a week or two of infection and may be accompanied by fatigue, headache, joint pain, and muscle aches. If it's left untreated, more severe symptoms can develop, including swelling in one or more joints, facial nerve palsy, and inflammation of the brain. Lyme disease can be treated with antibiotics.

Prompt removal of a tick reduces your chances of being infected, because it usually takes more than one day of the tick's sucking your blood for the bacteria to be transmitted to you. Unfortunately, nymphal (young) ticks are as small as a poppy seed, and you may not even notice having been bitten.

Lyme disease occurs across North America, Europe, and northern Asia. In the United States, about 20,000 cases are reported each year, according to the CDC. The disease is found across the United States, including Southern California, but more than 90 percent of reported cases are in the Northeast, plus Wisconsin and Minnesota.

Lizards may be a part of the explanation for the relative scarcity of Lyme disease in the western United States. When ticks feed on the blood of the western fence lizard, one of the most common lizards in California and surrounding areas, the ticks can be cleansed of the Lyme bacterium by a protein in the lizards' blood. Feeding on eastern fence lizards has also been shown to clear the Lyme pathogen from ticks, but eastern fence lizards are less important hosts for ticks than are their cousins in the west.

The CDC website is a good source of additional information on Lyme disease: http://www.cdc.gov/ncidod/dvbid/lyme/.

Oh, no—mono

What is mononucleosis, and what causes it?

Mononucleosis is an infectious disease with a triad of symptoms: fever, sore throat, and swollen lymph glands. It is caused by the Epstein-Barr virus (EBV), which belongs to a family of viruses that includes the virus that causes herpes. EBV is transmitted via saliva.

According to the CDC, EBV is one of the most common human viruses. The CDC estimates that up to 95 percent of adults have been infected with EBV by age 40. Infection with EBV often occurs in childhood (when the inadvertent sharing of drool among peers is not uncommon).

When infection with EBV occurs in childhood, symptoms usually are nonexistent or very mild. However, between one-third and one-half of EBV infections occurring during adolescence or young adulthood result in mononucleosis. Mononucleosis is most common in 15- to 17-year-olds, but it can occur at any age.

Most patients recover from mononucleosis within a month without medication. In rare cases, complications may include blood disorders, heart problems, neurological disorders, or rupture of the spleen.

Kitchen germs

Does putting all the dishes together in the sink (rather than running water and washing each dish individually) spread more germs than kill them? Use more water? Use more soap?

One study showed that people use between 6 and 30 gallons of water to hand-wash a load of dishes. Filling the sink with water and not letting the water run continuously used the least water. Hand-washing used more water on average (16 gallons) than a dishwasher (11 gallons). However, 60 percent of dishwasher users pre-rinse their dishes, which sends another 20 gallons down the drain. Soap use likely parallels water use.

Either method of hand-washing dishes has avoidable food safety pitfalls. Leaving dirty dishes to soak for a long time can allow bacteria to multiply. Sponges, cloths, and towels can harbor bacteria and should be changed often. Also, the Food and Drug Administration recommends that cutting boards used to cut raw meat be sanitized at a high temperature in a dishwasher or rinsed with a diluted solution of chlorine bleach.

Downers

The government says that the cow suffering from mad cow disease was found before it got into the food chain. However, did the disease strike the cow just before it was sent to slaughter, so that it was a "downed" animal, or was the disease developing for some time and could have entered the food chain if the cow was not a "downer"? Testing every cow, as they do in Japan, sounds like the best way to protect the beef we eat.

The cow, the second confirmed U.S. case of mad cow disease, or bovine spongiform encephalopathy (BSE), was a downer—too sickly to walk. Since inability to walk is a symptom of advanced BSE, the U.S.

Department of Agriculture targets downer cattle in its surveillance program, which tests about 1,000 cattle per day.

The USDA also bans downer cattle from the human food chain. (The cow in question was destined for pet food.) However, cattle can be infected with BSE long before they show any symptoms. In fact, the USDA has speculated that the 12-year-old cow may have become infected with BSE before the 1997 ban on feeding rendered meat and bonemeal to cows.

Stanley Prusiner, who won a Nobel Prize for discovering the cause of BSE and related diseases, argues that all slaughtered cattle should be tested for BSE. He thinks this is important for consumer safety and to provide insight into BSE—for example, to determine if new strains of the disease arise.

The USDA opposes universal testing. It even blocked one meatpacking company, Kansas-based Creekstone Farms, from testing every cow it slaughtered, which it wanted to do to maintain its beef exports to Japan. The USDA believed that permitting Creekstone to run its own tests would set an expensive precedent and force all meatpackers to do the same.

At $30 per animal, it would cost more than a billion dollars to test the 35 million cattle slaughtered annually in the United States. Universal testing would raise beef prices by approximately 5 cents per pound, a price most consumers would probably pay willingly if it ensured safety.

However, the USDA argues that it is not appropriate to test all cattle, because most cattle in this country are slaughtered between 18 and 20 months of age, and BSE is usually undetectable before 30 months.

In any case, new slaughtering practices, banning downer cattle, and increased surveillance mean that our beef is safer than it was back when our regulatory agencies did not believe BSE had reached American shores.

Mad cows

What is the latest research about how prions make cows or people mad?

Prions are proteins believed to cause mad cow disease (BSE) and its human equivalent, variant Creutzfeldt-Jakob disease (vCJD), as well as a number of other so-called prion diseases.

When it was initially proposed, the protein-only hypothesis—the idea that a protein on its own could cause disease—was considered preposterous, because a protein cannot replicate itself. Other disease-causing agents, including bacteria and viruses, have a genetic blueprint—DNA or RNA—which permits them to churn out copies of themselves.

Even after the 1997 Nobel Prize in Physiology or Medicine was awarded to Stanley Prusiner for research on prions as disease-causing agents, many scientists continued to believe that prion diseases were caused by an as-yet-undiscovered virus. Part of the continuing skepticism about the protein-only hypothesis resulted from scientists' inability to perform a key experiment: synthesize prion protein from scratch and show that this protein could cause neurological disease in animals.

Researchers had purified prions from the brain tissue of infected animals and had shown that they caused disease, but critics argued that the "purified" protein might not be completely free of DNA or RNA. The key experiment of synthesizing prions and showing that they can cause disease was finally done, and its publication, in *Science* in August 2004, silenced most of the skeptics.

As for how prions cause disease, scientists believe it has to do with protein folding. Prions, like other proteins, can bend into more than one shape. Prions in one shape are harmless, but in the other (infectious) shape they end up clumping together and damaging nerve cells. The word "spongiform" in BSE describes what the brain looks like (spongy) after prions wreak havoc.

In humans, and probably all vertebrates, normal prions are concentrated in the central nervous system. Their function is unknown, but one recent study suggests they may play a role in memory. Whatever their usual function, scientists think that when infectious prions come into contact with normal prions, they force the normal prions to refold into the infectious form. This sets up a chain reaction of refolding prions in the nervous system.

Many questions about prion diseases remain unanswered. Researchers are still trying to determine the length of time between consumption of infectious prions and the onset of symptoms of vCJD, what exactly happens in the body during that time, and what quantity of infectious prions is needed to cause illness. Another mystery is why prion diseases, including BSE, chronic wasting disease in deer and elk, and scrapie in sheep, differ in how easily they spread.

6

Assorted ailments

Two-faced warrior

It seems that those who have compromised immune systems, such as AIDS patients, are more vulnerable to both infectious diseases and certain types of cancer. Please explain what science currently knows about immunity to cancer relative to immunity to infectious diseases.

Our immune systems are trained to tolerate "self" and to attack invaders. Because cancer cells start out as normal cells in the body, the immune system tends to ignore them.

Nevertheless, many cancer cells have cancer-specific proteins on their surfaces, and efforts are under way to develop vaccines to teach patients' immune systems to recognize these proteins as foreign and to attack the cancer. Because cancer is not one disease, but more than 100 diseases characterized by the uncontrolled growth of cells, vaccines must be tailored for specific cancers.

In terms of how susceptibility to cancer is influenced by the state of one's immune system, research has revealed a paradox. On the one hand, people with AIDS and other conditions that suppress the immune system are more susceptible to cancers that are associated with infectious agents, such as human papillomavirus. Infectious conditions are thought to cause at least 15 percent of human cancers.

On the other hand, people with chronic inflammatory conditions—in which the immune system is overactive—also have a greater risk of getting cancer. Some chronic inflammatory disorders are triggered by infections, and others are genetic. Long-term usage of anti-inflammatory drugs has been shown to reduce cancer risk.

If the immune response simply consisted of Pac-Man-like immune cells gobbling up nasty invaders, a chronically "on" immune system would be more likely to find cancer cells and annihilate them. But the immune response also involves chemical warfare, which is effective against nasty microbes, but can also damage the DNA of healthy cells and cause them to become cancerous.

The immune system is not all about warmongering. It also plays a role in reconstruction efforts, and conditions that favor growth of normal cells also favor the growth of cancer cells. For example, angiogenesis—expansion of the network of blood vessels—is needed for wound repair, but it also provides the supply routes that nourish a growing tumor.

Further complicating the immune system and cancer story are reports in the older medical literature of acute infections—those triggering an "on/off" immune response—leading to spontaneous remission of tumors. Some historical cancer treatments involved injecting patients' tumors with bacterial toxins. One analogous conventional therapy is approved by the U.S. Food and Drug Administration. It uses a live bacterium, applied directly to the tumor, in the treatment of bladder cancer.

Pimple food

Why do chocolate and oily foods produce acne?

Isaac Asimov once said, "The first law of dietetics seems to be: If it tastes good, it's bad for you." Teenagers will probably find that Asimov's words echo the advice they receive on diet and acne—advice that is a blend of truth and folklore.

Acne is less prevalent in rural, nonindustrialized societies. For example, acne was absent in Inuit people when they were following traditional ways of living and eating. After their transition to modern life, the prevalence of acne became similar to that in Western societies.

Some scientists have therefore speculated that acne is caused by high-glycemic diets—diets high in sugar and refined starches—which are typical of adolescents in Westernized societies. They hypothesize that frequent consumption of high-glycemic food leads to chronically elevated insulin. High insulin may initiate a hormone cascade that leads to overproduction of skin cells in pores and results in blockages.

It is a tantalizing hypothesis, but testing it satisfactorily requires getting large numbers of people to change their diets radically for a significant period of time. At least one such study is under way.

Studies of the effect on acne of *individual* foods, including sugary foods like chocolate and greasy foods like French fries and pizza, typically have found no relationship between consumption of the food and acne. Chocolate has been vindicated in several studies.

Milk was implicated in one recent study, in which women were grouped according to how many milk products they recalled consuming as teens. In the highest-consumption group, a slightly higher percentage of women had had severe acne as teens compared to the lowest-consumption group. The researchers speculated that the many hormones that occur naturally in milk could cause acne. However, this study does not prove that milk causes acne. It is equally possible that acne causes milk consumption—due to pressure by family members telling acne sufferers that drinking milk will clear up their skin.

Dermatologists think that iodine sensitivity may be responsible for a small number of cases of acne. Iodine in kelp, shellfish, and certain mineral supplements could irritate pores in sensitive individuals. Incidentally, milk also contains iodine from supplements fed to cows and sanitizing solutions used on udders.

So although a healthy diet is good advice for everyone, and some people may have sensitivities to certain foods, acne is a complex disease. No compelling evidence exists that any one food is a complexion nightmare.

Much ado about nothing

What causes allergies? Why are some people allergic to certain substances while others are not?

The National Institute of Allergy and Infectious Diseases reports that allergies affect more than 50 million Americans and cost the health care system $18 billion annually.

An allergic reaction occurs when the body mobilizes defenses against a harmless substance. On encountering an allergen such as grass pollen, immune cells in the body of an allergy-prone individual manufacture large amounts of a type of antibody called IgE.

IgE antibodies attach themselves to mast cells, which usually produce chemicals in response to invading microbes. When the IgE antibodies encounter the allergen they recognize, they stimulate the mast cells to produce chemicals, including histamine, which act on the blood vessels, mucous glands, and other organs and produce the symptoms of the specific allergic condition.

Common respiratory allergens are pollen, mold spores, dust mites, and animal fur and dander. Latex, insect bites, drugs (for instance, penicillin), and jewelry can also cause allergic reactions. Common food allergens are milk, eggs, nuts, wheat, and seafood.

Not all food intolerances are allergies. For example, many people lack an enzyme needed to break down lactose—a sugar found in milk. Lactose intolerance is different from an allergy, which involves producing antibodies to a component of milk. Even so, the symptoms of food intolerances and allergies can be similar.

Researchers have estimated that more than 50 genes influence people's susceptibility to developing allergies. For example, some people have an inherited tendency to produce excessive amounts of the IgE antibody. Hay fever, asthma, eczema, and food allergies are common in these families.

Nongenetic factors play an important role as well. For example, infants who have been breastfed are less likely to develop allergies. Psychological stress has been shown to aggravate allergy symptoms.

The "hygiene hypothesis" was introduced to explain the rising incidence of allergies in Western societies ever more obsessed with cleanliness. It suggests that exposure to airborne allergens and microbes early in life prevents our immune systems from becoming overly sensitive, reducing allergy risk. However, the hypothesis fails to explain the high rates of asthma and allergies in youth exposed to inner-city air pollution.

With respect to food allergens, frequent, early exposure may increase allergy risk. For example, rice allergy is more common in children in Japan, and fish allergy is more common in Scandinavia. Researchers think this is because children have more porous or "leaky" intestines than adults, making it easier for proteins to get into the bloodstream and initiate an immune reaction.

Hiccups attacking

Why do we hiccup?

Hiccups are involuntary contractions of the diaphragm—the main muscle used for breathing. The resulting intake of air is abruptly interrupted by the closing of the glottis—the opening between the vocal cords—leading to the characteristic sound.

Eating too fast or anything else that can trigger a sudden spasm of the diaphragm can cause hiccups. They are more likely to occur when the stomach is stretched following a meal. Certain medical conditions can also cause hiccups, such as a stroke that interferes with the part of the brain that regulates breathing, or an irritation of the diaphragm due to pneumonia.

Opinions vary on whether hiccups serve any purpose. One proposal is that hiccups are an evolutionary by-product of respiratory behaviors in lower vertebrates. Another is that the hiccup may help open the sphincter—a ring-like band of muscle—in the lower esophagus, permitting the escape of gas from the stomach and thus relieving pressure.

Attacking hiccups

Why does taking a lump of sugar with a few drops of raspberry-flavored vinegar stop hiccups? (That is my son's cure, and it has never failed. We have never tried it with plain or any other type of vinegar.)

There are many folk remedies for hiccups. Some of them, such as drinking from the far side of a glass, may be more interesting to watch than effective. Interrupting the normal respiratory cycle by holding your breath or being startled (gasping) sometimes provides relief. So can stimulating the back of the throat, as happens when you swallow a lump of sugar. The resulting nerve impulses must shut down the hiccup circuitry.

Presumably these home remedies did not work for Charles Osborne, who made it into *Guinness World Records* for his 68-year attack of hiccups.

Gulp

If the sensation of a lump in the throat is referred to as globus syndrome or globus hystericus only if medical tests rule out injury or disease as a possible cause, what kinds of injury or disease could cause the sensation?

When there is a physical rather than psychological explanation for the enduring sensation of a lump in the throat, globus hystericus is not the correct diagnosis. Unfortunately, it is common for people to be misdiagnosed with the syndrome. One study, in which extensive medical tests were conducted on 231 patients who had been diagnosed with globus hystericus, revealed that 80 percent of them had physical conditions responsible for the sensation.

A surprisingly wide range of disorders can cause the uncomfortable sensation of a mass in the throat. The most obvious is a real mass—a benign or cancerous tumor. The sensation can also result from neurological disorders, such as degenerative diseases or damage from a stroke. Low blood sugar and electrolyte disturbances—low levels of calcium, potassium, magnesium, or sodium—may also be responsible.

Another possibility is gastroesophageal reflux disease, or acid reflux. One study employed catheters to measure the acidity along the length of the esophagus of patients with the globus sensation. It showed that acid reflux limited to the lower third of the esophagus could cause the sensation. The researchers speculated that the vagus nerve could transmit the irritation from the lower to upper esophagus. Treatment for acid reflux relieved the globus sensation in the majority of these patients.

An extensive list of possible physical causes for throat lumps can be found in "Globus Hystericus: A Brief Review," a paper in the journal *General Hospital Psychiatry*, volume 26 (2004).

Knee forecast

I've heard it said that when the barometer falls, people have increased joint pain and claim that the pressure caused the pain. What exactly does this mean?

Barometric pressure is the force of the atmosphere pushing down at a particular location. Pressure is higher where air is slowly descending and lower where it is slowly rising. Low pressure often brings precipitation because air cools as it rises and the moisture in it condenses. High pressure usually is associated with clear weather, because the warming of air as it descends hampers the formation of clouds.

In addition, atmospheric pressure is lower at higher elevations because there are fewer air molecules. On weather maps, air pressure is adjusted to factor out altitude. This adjustment reveals the more subtle differences in pressure associated with movements of air that influence weather conditions.

The belief that weather and physical well-being are linked is longstanding. Hippocrates wrote about it in the fifth century B.C. "Wind wet" is the literal translation of the Chinese characters for rheumatism.

The majority of patients with joint inflammation report that their condition is affected by weather. Some claim that the aches in their joints provide an accurate weather forecast. There may be some truth to this, but researchers are still puzzling over the exact relationship between weather and joint ailments.

For example, according to some studies, patients' joint symptoms flare up when barometric pressure is higher. Other studies have found the exact opposite. Still other studies suggest that joint pain worsens only when the pressure changes. Cold weather was also typically found to aggravate symptoms, as was increased humidity. Some studies have found that decreased sunlight and increased wind speed worsen symptoms.

The reason for the variability in the research findings is unclear. It may be due to differences in patient populations. The different types of arthritis and other joint problems may respond to weather in different ways. Then again, it may depend on the geographic location in which the study was carried out. Different combinations of weather variables may play a role in different climates.

Several possible mechanisms could account for the effects of weather on pain. Changes in temperature or pressure could make nerve endings more sensitive. Alternatively, because ligaments, tendons, bones, muscles, and scar tissue are all different densities, atmospheric changes could cause pain by contracting and expanding these tissues differentially. Weather patterns also affect mood in some people, which can alter pain perception.

Brain whittling

What is the most common way people lose brain cells?

Surprisingly, neither disease nor trauma wipes out the greatest number of brain cells. The grimmest reaper in our brains is normal development. In some parts of the nervous system, it wipes out half the total number of nerve cells generated.

During development, the number of nerve cells rises to a maximum as cells proliferate and migrate to their final destinations. Nerve cells send out "feelers" called growth cones to find one another and form connections. Cells that fail to make appropriate connections are tidily eliminated.

Although this process may seem wasteful, it permits much more flexibility than would be possible if every nerve cell and connection were specified by our genes. Instead, it provides a mechanism through which brain anatomy and function in humans and other complex animals can respond to environmental influences.

The form of cell death that neatly eliminates unwanted cells is apoptosis. The term is derived from a Greek root that means "dropping of leaves off a tree." During apoptosis cells shrink and display signals on their surfaces that tell other cells to eat them. Neighboring cells or white blood cells known as macrophages engulf the dying cells. Apoptosis is carefully controlled and does not injure the surrounding tissue.

In contrast, following infection, stroke, or trauma (such as when a big rock conks Wile E. Coyote on the head), brain cells mainly die via necrosis. Necrosis is much messier than apoptosis. It involves the leakage of cell contents and inflammation, which can damage nearby cells.

This is not to say that apoptosis is always a good thing. Sometimes apoptosis gets activated abnormally. For example, exposing the developing brain to alcohol can activate apoptosis and delete millions of nerve cells. The resulting damage is responsible for the most disabling features of fetal alcohol syndrome.

Evidence is mounting that apoptosis also plays an important role in many disorders characterized by slow degeneration of the central nervous system, such as Lou Gehrig's disease (ALS), Parkinson's disease, Huntington's disease, and Alzheimer's disease. Therefore, a great deal of research is directed at understanding what cellular signals activate apoptosis.

In modern society, the most common cause of intellectual deterioration is Alzheimer's. In the United States, about 2 percent of the population is affected, but more than half of individuals over age 85 may have the disease, according to an article in the *American Journal of Medicine*. Cell numbers may decline by 20 to 80 percent in certain regions of the brain over the course of one or two decades as the disease progresses.

Head bop

What happens in the brain of a boxer that causes him to lose consciousness and fall to the mat after a blow to the head?

The fluid surrounding the brain helps cushion it during everyday activities, but blows to the head create mechanical stress on brain tissue. When nerve cells are forcibly stretched and compressed, channels open in the outer membranes of the nerve cells. Ions can then flood into the cells and create a sudden electric discharge, which can result in loss of consciousness.

The electric discharge also leads to the release of neurotransmitters—chemicals nerve cells use to talk to one another. Excessive release of neurotransmitters can injure nerve cells. Damage can also result directly from the shearing strain on brain tissue. Brain scans have revealed that the longer the period of unconsciousness following the blow to the head, the deeper the location of the lesions in the brain.

Approximately 20 percent of professional boxers suffer from chronic traumatic brain injury (CTBI). Symptoms of CTBI are impairments in thought, behavior, and muscle control. When the symptoms are severe, CTBI is known as dementia pugilistica or punch-drunk syndrome. As in Alzheimer's, the brains of people with CTBI accumulate senile plaques (abnormal deposits of protein) and tangles (twisted bundles of fibers).

Cappuccino compulsion

How do people become addicted to caffeine?

In North America, 80 to 90 percent of adults use caffeine on a regular basis. The average daily intake among caffeine consumers is 280 milligrams, equivalent to drinking a large mug of coffee and a couple cans of cola. Some studies have shown that drinking as little as one cup of coffee per day can result in caffeine addiction. On the other hand, based on how caffeine affects the brain, some researchers dispute the notion that caffeine is addictive.

Addictive drugs such as cocaine and amphetamines act on the brain's reward system. In humans and other animals, the normal function of the brain's reward system is to generate pleasurable feelings to reinforce behaviors that support survival. By artificially activating reward system structures—specifically, the nucleus accumbens, ventral tegmental area, and prefrontal cortex—drugs hijack the reward system.

At normal doses, caffeine stimulates the prefrontal cortex, but not the other regions of the brain's reward system. So caffeine's action on the brain does not look like that of a typical addictive drug. Nevertheless, the withdrawal symptoms that many people experience when deprived of their java can motivate the regular use of caffeine and make it difficult to kick the habit.

In experimental studies, 50 percent of people got headaches when they stopped using caffeine, and 13 percent had withdrawal symptoms serious enough to impair their ability to function normally. In addition to headaches, symptoms of caffeine withdrawal include fatigue, difficulty concentrating, depression, irritability, nausea, and muscle pain. Symptoms usually begin within 12 hours of ceasing caffeine consumption and last for up to a week.

Caffeine initially increases heart rate and alertness because it blocks the action of adenosine, a natural chemical in the body that inhibits nerve activity. Adenosine opens blood vessels, and caffeine constricts them. That is why caffeine is found in some headache medications, such as Anacin; caffeine relieves some headaches by reducing the volume of blood in the brain.

The body responds to regular caffeine exposure by increasing the activity of adenosine. Drowsiness and headaches occur when one abruptly cuts out caffeine because caffeine is no longer around to counteract the effects of adenosine. Gradually reducing caffeine intake gives the body time to adjust and results in fewer withdrawal symptoms than going cold turkey.

The good news is that as long as caffeine is not keeping you awake at night, little evidence exists to suggest that caffeine consumption is harmful to your health.

Many malignancies

Is there such a thing as heart cancer? I've never read anything about it.

Yes. From autopsy data it is estimated that heart cancer afflicts between one in 10,000 to one in 100,000 people. Since it is very rare, it does not get much media attention. Similarly, we do not usually hear about male breast cancer, but around 1 percent of all breast cancers occur in men.

According to the World Health Organization, 10 million people are diagnosed with cancer annually. The most common cancers worldwide are cancers of the skin (approximately one-third of newly diagnosed cancer cases), lung cancer (12 percent), breast cancer (10 percent), and cancer of the rectum/colon (9 percent). Cancers of the stomach, prostate, liver, cervix, esophagus, bladder, lymph nodes, blood (leukemia), and mouth/throat are the next most common types of cancer.

The majority of cancers originate in epithelial cells, which form the outer layers of the skin and line the digestive, respiratory, reproductive, and urinary systems. Because epithelial cells divide very quickly (relative to muscle cells, for example), ample opportunity exists for something to go awry. The heart is mainly muscle tissue, and most cases of heart cancer are due to tumors that originated in other parts of the body (for example, in the lung or breast) and spread to the heart.

New skin

Our skin cells are continually dying, sloughing off, and being replaced by new cells. Why do we get skin cancer from sun-damaged skin when those damaged cells are being replaced continually by new cells?

The outer layer of our skin—the stratum corneum—consists of dead skin cells called keratinocytes. As you point out, these cells are constantly being shed and replaced by keratinocytes from deeper layers. A keratinocyte lives for about a month, but cancer often takes many years to develop, because a cell accumulates on average five mutations before becoming cancerous. Indeed, skin cancer would be much more prevalent if skin cells were not replaced so frequently.

The three most common forms of skin cancer are melanoma, basal cell carcinoma, and squamous cell carcinoma. Melanoma is cancer of the melanocytes—the cells that produce the dark pigment melanin in our skin. Melanocytes are not replaced rapidly like the keratinocytes. However, basal cell carcinoma and squamous cell carcinoma are cancers of the keratinocytes. Scientists now believe these two forms of skin cancer arise in keratinocyte stem cells.

One characteristic of a stem cell is that it renews itself when it divides. When a keratinocyte stem cell divides, one of the two daughter cells eventually makes its way to the skin surface and flakes off, but the other remains behind as a stem cell. If the parent stem cell had mutations, these are passed along to each daughter cell. The daughter stem cell (or its descendants) can reside in the skin long enough to accumulate multiple mutations and become cancerous.

On the mend

A year ago I was diagnosed with Type 2 diabetes. I was started on medication. I also began a program of diet and exercise. As of today I have lost 60 pounds and, with my doctor's approval, have stopped taking diabetes medication. My last blood sugar test was in the normal range. Do I still have diabetes?

A basic dictionary definition—to cure is to restore to health—implies that your diabetes is cured, but this definition is deficient when it comes to complex diseases. According to Steve Edelman, a diabetes specialist at the University of California San Diego School of Medicine, your diabetes is totally controlled, but not cured. We do not yet have a cure for diabetes. If you regained the weight, your diabetes would return, which would not be the case if your diabetes were truly cured.

Even for infectious diseases, the definition of *cure* is not straightforward. According to Francesca Torriani, an infectious-disease specialist at the UC San Diego School of Medicine, a cure means that no signs of infection (sickness, inflammation) are evident and that the tests for the disease agent are negative. However, some people who test positive for a bacterium or virus never become ill, because people's susceptibility and immunity influence who gets an infection.

Cancer is arguably the most difficult disease to classify as cured, because cancer is not a single disease, but a collection of more than 100 different diseases. According to Greg Daniels, a melanoma expert at the UC San Diego Moores Cancer Center, curing cancer means that the cancer is no longer there and it never comes back.

He points out that this definition is retrospective. Two patients with the same cancer, given the same treatment, who seem to respond equally well in the short term, may fare differently in the long term. For example, treatment for Stage 1 melanoma cures 90 percent of patients, but 10 percent will have a recurrence. Until a recurrence happens, the cured and uncured patients are indistinguishable.

Even the first part of the definition—no longer there—is tricky, because it depends on the sensitivity of the tests for that cancer. PET scans and CAT scans make it possible to detect clusters of billions of cancer cells, but a cluster of a million cells would not be visible.

Therefore, for all diseases, signs of the disease must be absent before a patient can be considered cured, but concluding that a disease is cured often requires the test of time. Some diseases, although treatable, are incurable.

Flakiness

What exactly is dandruff? Why doesn't it spread to a person's eyebrows, mustache, or beard? And, most of all, what makes it itchy?

For more than 100 years, a fungus called *Malassezia* has been implicated in dandruff. Puzzlingly, however, *Malassezia* is found naturally on all of us, and people with dandruff do not have more of it than people without dandruff. Only recently did scientists discover how otherwise-harmless microorganisms cause dandruff in some people but not others.

Malassezia feasts on sebum, the oil produced by the skin. Sebum is a mixture of many different oily, fatty, and waxy substances. The scalp is not the only place the fungus can get a free lunch, so dandruff can occur elsewhere, including eyebrows, forehead, and behind the ears. *Malassezia* is a picky eater, consuming only certain fats and releasing broken-down fats as waste products. In doing so, the fungus changes the composition of skin oils.

Sebum usually lubricates and protects the skin, but a recent study determined that applying waste fats produced by the fungus to the scalps of dandruff-prone people caused irritation and skin flaking. Under a microscope the skin flakes looked like normal dandruff. On the other hand, individuals who were not dandruff-susceptible did not get dandruff when the fats produced by *Malassezia* were applied to their scalps.

The researchers concluded that the skin of dandruff sufferers is more permeable than that of non-dandruff sufferers, which allows the fats from *Malassezia* to irritate the skin, leading to itchiness and excess turnover of scalp cells. Changes in the skin's permeability could also explain why some people suddenly develop dandruff when they are under stress or have a weakened immune system.

The occurrence of dandruff during development and maturity follows the pattern of sebum production, which is under hormonal control. The glands that produce sebum are active at birth under the control of maternal hormones. This allows initial *Malassezia* colonization. *Malassezia* is likely an irritating factor for cradle cap, a scalp flaking disorder in infants.

The glands then get smaller and decrease sebum production, causing *Malassezia* populations to decline along with the incidence of dandruff, until puberty. Sebum production drops again after menopause in women and after age 50 or 60 in men.

Dandruff is prevalent, affecting more than 50 percent of adults. Active ingredients in the many antidandruff shampoos differ, but antifungal activity usually is the common mechanism of action.

Charley horse

What causes recurring muscle cramps? Are there ways to prevent them?

Cramps can occur due to an imbalance of a lot of things, such as calcium and potassium, according to Joseph Scherger, a professor and physician at the University of California San Diego School of Medicine. He recommends that people suffering from cramps see their primary care physician, who, after initial tests, might refer them to a rheumatologist—a doctor who specializes in disorders of the joints and muscles.

A search of the medical literature turns up a long list of possible causes of muscle cramps. In addition to imbalances of electrolytes (magnesium, calcium, potassium, sodium) and dehydration, cramps can occur as a side effect of certain medications and as a symptom of many diseases, including diabetes, thyroid disease, and peripheral vascular disease—narrowing of the blood vessels, especially in the legs.

Treating an underlying disease would be the first course of action in eliminating muscle cramps. However, muscle cramps often turn out to be "idiopathic"—of unknown cause.

To prevent cramps, the authors of the *Harvard Health Letter* recommend staying hydrated, especially because, as we get older, our thirst impulse gets weaker, and we may forget to drink. In addition, they report that the average American does not consume an adequate amount of potassium. They recommend almonds and fruits and vegetables including bananas, oranges, spinach, lettuce, and mushrooms as good sources of potassium.

They also suggest wearing comfortable, supportive shoes, stretching your muscles regularly, and making sure your bed covers are not too snug. Tight covers can press on your feet and tighten the muscles in your calf and foot. Tight muscles are more susceptible to cramping.

Medications and vitamin E, which has proven helpful in some studies, are other options that patients might explore in consultation with their doctors.

Throbbin' noggin

What makes the head ache during a headache? What is different with a migraine?

Headaches come in a surprising variety, with different causes and mechanisms. The latest diagnostic classification by the International Headache Society lists well over 200 kinds of headaches, including the tension-type headache, the migraine, the cluster headache, the alcohol-induced headache, and the headache attributed to ingestion of a cold stimulus—the ice cream headache to you and me.

"You make my brain hurt" is a favorite retort to an annoying person in comics and comedies, but brain tissue does not feel pain. A patient can be awake during brain surgery (allowing the surgeon to monitor what is safe to cut) and not feel the knife. Headaches arise from other structures in the head and neck, including skin, joints, muscles, sinuses, and the blood vessels in the dura mater—a tough covering around the brain.

The tension-type headache is the kind most everyone has experienced. Nevertheless, its mechanism is not well understood. The old idea that it results from involuntary muscle contractions that block blood flow to the head has been ruled out, but it may have something to do with "a pain in the neck." Frequent sufferers of tension-type headaches experience increased tenderness of the neck muscles and tendons. Another, albeit controversial, hypothesis is that a tension-type headache is an earlier, less severe phase of a migraine, and that they share a similar mechanism.

Migraines affect 18 percent of women and 6 percent of men each year. The World Health Organization lists migraines among the top 20 causes of disability worldwide. Migraines are severe, often throbbing headaches that intensify with physical activity, and they may be accompanied by nausea and aversion to strong light, smells, or sounds. In some people the migraine is preceded by an aura—neurological symptoms such as flashing lights, blind spots, or numbness.

A migraine begins with a wave of decreased nerve activity that moves across the brain's cortex (surface layer). The decreased nerve activity, also known as the cortical spreading depression (CSD), initiates many changes in the levels of chemicals that brain cells use to communicate with each other and dilates the blood vessels in the dura mater. The swelling blood vessels stretch the nerves around them, causing them to send signals to the trigeminal nerve, which relays pain messages in the face and head.

Stress, certain foods, sleep disruptions, skipping meals, and hormonal changes can trigger migraines. Exactly how these factors trigger the CSD, and why the triggers are different for different people, is not yet understood.

Heart hurt

What causes the nausea associated with heart attacks?

A region in the brain stem that receives input from the body and other parts of the brain coordinates vomiting. Being able to detect and reject toxins inadvertently consumed with food has an obvious adaptive advantage for an organism. Therefore, it is not surprising that the digestive tract contains sense organs to detect noxious chemicals and convey that information to the brain.

Sense organs that affect nausea are also found in the chest area, including the heart and lungs. Exposing the heart to certain chemicals, mechanically distending it, or electrically stimulating the right cardiac nerve can initiate reflexes involved in vomiting. Sense organs in the left ventricle of the heart that detect tension appear to trigger the nausea associated with heart attacks.

The adaptive benefit of this nausea response is unclear. However, since these same sense organs in the heart may be responsible for the nausea that sometimes accompanies heavy exercise, perhaps their role is to serve as a warning to an organism to prevent fatal overexertion.

Knowing thyself

My sister has lupus. One of the tests the doctors did was an antinuclear antibodies (ANA) test, which detected antibodies to her cell nuclear contents. But aren't the nuclear contents contained in two membranes (cell and nuclear), so the white blood cells should have no contact with them? Can the white blood cells tell the self DNA apart from non-self DNA?

DNA and other contents of the cell's nucleus are indeed carefully contained within healthy cells. In contrast, when cells die, the contents of the nucleus are often released. So our white blood cells—which defend us against invading microbes—do come into contact with DNA from our body's cells (self DNA).

White blood cells produce protein weapons called antibodies that bind to and neutralize invaders. White blood cells are skilled warriors and make different antibody weapons for different intruders. Therefore, blood tests for many diseases work by identifying specific antibodies in the blood.

For 40 years, the ANA test has been used to help diagnose lupus. Despite the test's long history, two things remain puzzling. First, if everyone's white blood cells come into contact with self DNA, why doesn't everyone have antibodies against it? It turns out that we do, but the antibodies are present in much smaller amounts, and bind to DNA much more weakly, than the anti-DNA antibodies found in lupus patients.

The second puzzle is whether these antibodies play a role in causing the symptoms of lupus. In systemic lupus, the body's immune system attacks its own tissues, including the joints and internal organs. Antibodies would not harm the body by simply binding to DNA released by dying cells.

Researchers have found that the antibodies tend to collect in the kidneys of lupus patients, where they may penetrate into cells. The exact role of these antibodies in lupus remains under investigation.

White blood cells can tell the difference between self and non-self DNA, or at least between DNA from bacteria versus DNA from mammals. Since the DNA building blocks, or bases, used by bacteria (A, T, G, C) are the same as the ones that make up our genes, this is surprising.

However, although the building blocks are the same, the way they are strung together is different. Specifically, bacteria have many more sequences that are particularly rich in C and G bases than we do. Also, in us this sequence is more likely to be modified by the addition of four atoms called a methyl group. These features allow white blood cells to distinguish bacterial DNA from our DNA.

Halo of stars

I've always wanted to know what causes the sensation of seeing stars. Today, after swimming laps, I was lying in the sun. As I opened my eyes, about to get up, I saw intermittent small white dots buzzing around for about 30 seconds. My best guess is that it has something to do with oxygen. Can you shed some light on this for me?

There are at least three possible reasons for seeing stars. Sylvester the cat saw stars when Granny walloped him over the head for trying to eat Tweety Bird. A blow to the head can cause the vitreous fluid that fills the back two-thirds of the eyeball to rub against the retina. In fact, as we age, the vitreous fluid becomes thicker and can push or pull on the retina even with more modest movements of the head.

The retina does not feel pain; it just responds to stimulation by sending a light signal, according David Granet, a professor of ophthalmology at the University of California San Diego School of Medicine. Certain types of exertion cause the "stars" by stimulating the retina. "Of course, a shower of stars, flashing light, or a curtain on vision are all potential warning signs of retinal detachment and should be of concern," he said.

Injury to the retina should be treated immediately to minimize further tearing and bleeding into the eye. If the damage is not too extensive, retinas can be repaired with a laser on an outpatient basis.

Another reason for seeing stars is small clumps of gel that form in the vitreous fluid. These "floaters" cast a shadow on the retina when they pass in front of it and are most obvious when you are looking at a plain, light-colored background.

The third reason for seeing stars has to do with levels of oxygen and/or nutrients reaching the brain. According to Joseph Scherger, a professor and physician at the UC San Diego School of Medicine, "The brain, including vision, runs on glucose, oxygen, a balance of electrolytes, and ample circulation/blood pressure. One might have visual changes like 'stars' if any of these are low."

Hot, hot, hot

I asked my physician if the temperature of a hot flash can be measured and what it might be, and he said he didn't know. I've tried with my home thermometer, and it always reads normal, but I don't feel normal! Can you measure the temperature of a hot flash? If so, how? Where in the body does the signal for a hot flash originate?

Hot flashes seem to be triggered by an overly sensitive body thermostat. A useful analogy is a house thermostat that is adjusted so that a temperature increase of a fraction of a degree switches on the air conditioning. A false alarm, such as a waft of heat from opening the oven door, could activate the air conditioning, but since the house was not overly warm to begin with, the AC would rapidly turn off.

When the body's thermostat, which is located in the hypothalamus of the brain, decides it is too hot, it cranks on the body's air conditioning—sweating and dilation of blood vessels in the skin. The rush of warm blood to the skin creates the feeling of intense heat characteristic of the hot flash. If the ambient temperature is not actually high, our AC quickly shuts down. The blood vessels in the skin constrict, and the blood drains away, leaving the skin pale and cold.

Studies have shown that, on average, women who experience hot flashes have a lower core body temperature and a lower sweating threshold—that is, they begin sweating at a lower body temperature—than women who do not experience hot flashes. However, the temperature difference is small, just a fraction of a degree, and therefore requires a very sensitive thermometer to measure.

The standard explanation for the occurrence of hot flashes during menopause is that they are triggered by declining levels of estrogen. Estrogen has been shown to ameliorate hot flashes by increasing the sweating threshold. It is not understood how declining estrogen levels increase the sensitivity of the nerve cells in the brain that control body temperature.

Although considered the hallmark of the menopausal transition, hot flashes can occur at other times of life and can affect both women and men. Also, not all women experience hot flashes during menopause. Research is ongoing to determine if other hormones are involved, and to identify health and lifestyle factors that might increase a woman's risk of having hot flashes.

7

Uniquely human

Odd eats

Why do humans cook food, and when did they start doing this? Do any other animals modify their food intake?

Early humans probably first realized the value of cooked food when they tasted tubers—root vegetables like potatoes and cassava—that had been roasted by a lightning-sparked grass fire. Not only are cooked tubers more delectable, but heat alters the structure of starches and proteins, making them easier to digest and rendering some poisonous vegetables edible.

How long ago humans were able to control fire is still under dispute. By 250,000 years ago, our ancestors could certainly invite the neighbors over for a barbeque. Across Europe and the Middle East, ancient earthen ovens with burned animal bones date from that time. Some anthropologists argue that humans controlled fire almost 2 million years ago. They point to circular areas of scorched earth almost that old discovered in Africa. These "bonfires" contained a mixture of burned wood types, which suggests that they were deliberately set, rather than the remains of a tree struck by lightning.

Wild and domesticated animals can learn to distinguish a food's nutritional properties based on its appearance, smell, or taste. Animals modify their diets according to how their nutritional needs change as they mature, during pregnancy and lactation, and as a result of disease. Zoopharmacognosy—self-medication by animals—is a particularly intriguing aspect of diet modification.

Ill animals of many different species consume things that normally are not a part of their diets but that have medicinal properties. These include laxatives, antidiarrheals, antibiotics, antiparasitics, and antidotes to toxins they have previously consumed. For example, wild chimpanzees with parasitic infections eat leaves from a shrub commonly known as bitter leaf. The leaves contain several chemicals that can kill parasites that cause malaria and other tropical infections.

Many animals eat soil—a habit known as geophagy. Soil is a source of minerals. Geophagy is also a form of zoopharmacognosy. Soil containing certain types of clay combats diarrhea. By binding to toxic plant compounds, soil makes some plants safer to eat. Soil also can enhance plants' pharmacological activities by binding to interfering compounds.

A study showed that zoopharmacognosy requires learning; it is not purely instinctive. In the study, lambs were given food laced with one of three chemicals that cause stomachaches. Then they were given a choice of three medicines, each of which would cure a stomachache caused by only one of the chemicals. Only lambs that had prior experience being cured by the appropriate medicine could select it when given the choice of all three.

Sink like a stone

Humans, as primates, typically learn how to swim when they're old enough to follow instructions from swimmers. Can any other primates swim instinctively? What other mammal species do not swim instinctively?

I remember being surprised as a child to learn that our cat could swim very well, although he much preferred *terra firma*. Many land mammals can swim, and they tend to use a similar gait in water as they do on land.

It is difficult to know for sure what mammals cannot swim, since many avoid water if given the choice. However, rats, mice, horses, elephants, camels, bears, antelope, skunks, at least some species of bats, and at least one species of armadillo reportedly can swim.

According to the San Diego Zoo's Associate Curator of Mammals, Karen Killmar, most monkeys can probably swim. This behavior has not been documented in all species but has been seen in many. In contrast, there are no reports of great apes (gorillas, chimpanzees, orangutans) swimming. They have been observed in the wild wading in deep water, but not actually swimming. Most researchers do not believe that these species have swimming as an instinctive behavior.

A word of caution to pet owners: Some dogs do not like to swim, and they may panic in deep water, especially if a steep bank makes it difficult for them to climb out. And, of course, a strong current can fatigue even the best swimmer, canine or otherwise.

Dino breath

Not considering the millions of years dividing their times on Earth, am I mistaken in thinking that humans could not have survived in the oxygen content of the air during the dinosaur era?

Dinosaurs roamed the Earth from about 230 million years ago to about 65 million years ago. Estimates of the oxygen levels during the dinosaurs' reign differ greatly, but a 2005 study published in the journal *Science* found that the atmosphere's oxygen concentration has increased over the last 205 million years from 10 percent to 21 percent.

Another study found evidence that about 240 million years ago, oxygen concentrations dropped precipitously and rapidly from about 35 percent to about 12 percent. Therefore, based on these two studies, dinosaurs survived in an oxygen concentration as low as about half of today's levels.

Today, at high or low elevations, 21 percent of the molecules in the air are oxygen, but fewer air molecules (in a specific volume of air) are present at higher elevations. On the Andean and Tibetan plateaus, about 13,000 feet (4 kilometers) above sea level, each breath you take would contain about as many oxygen molecules as it would if taken at sea level back in the time of the earliest dinosaurs.

Humans can survive under these low-oxygen conditions. In fact, some Andean miners live for long periods at nearly 20,000 feet, where there is even less oxygen.

Just because human populations can survive at these lower oxygen concentrations does not mean that oxygen levels had no role in the evolution of mammals. Small mammals coexisted with dinosaurs. However, the *Science* paper reported that a dramatic increase in the size and diversity of mammals occurred between 100 and 65 million years ago, during a period of relatively high and stable oxygen levels.

The paper's authors think that the increase in oxygen levels may have facilitated the evolution of large mammals. Larger mammals have fewer blood vessels per unit of muscle than smaller mammals. As a result, larger mammals need higher levels of oxygen in the environment to achieve maximum rates of metabolism.

Dinosaurs may have had lower rates of metabolism, and lower oxygen needs, than mammals. In addition, a group of dinosaurs that includes the brontosaurus is thought to have had a respiratory system similar to that of modern birds, with a series of air sacs that act like bellows to move air through the lungs. The system allows fresh air to flow through the lungs continuously and could have given dinosaurs a survival advantage in low-oxygen conditions.

Modern man

Has the* Homo sapiens *species stopped evolving due to our scientific progress in overcoming the survival of the fittest, or are we still undergoing small changes that are not easily perceived?

The *Homo sapiens* species has existed about 200,000 years, but just 10,000 years ago the transition from hunter-gatherer to agricultural societies created significant evolutionary pressures. Specifically, diet changed, and the spread of infectious diseases increased as population densities increased.

By comparing the genomes of various modern individuals, geneticists can determine how quickly our DNA sequences have been changing, and whether the changes are random or result from some sort of evolutionary pressure.

One interesting example is the gene for lactase. Lactase breaks down lactose, the main sugar in milk. A version of the gene that permits adults to digest lactose is prevalent in people of European ancestry and some African populations but is very rare in Southeast Asian and sub-Saharan African populations. The geographic distribution and timing of the gene's increase in prevalence correspond to the rise of dairy farming.

Other genes that have changed in one or more populations as a result of relatively recent (over the past 10,000 years) evolutionary pressures include genes that play a role in metabolism, taste and smell, fertility, and skin pigmentation.

In developing nations, where AIDS, malaria, and other scourges kill millions every year, genes that provide resistance to disease are under selection pressure. For example, in regions of the world where malaria is or was recently found, certain versions of genes for hemoglobin—the oxygen-carrying protein in the blood—have become prevalent. These versions of the gene provide some resistance to malaria but can cause blood diseases such as sickle cell anemia.

Some scientists have argued that in developed countries, evolutionary pressures have been relaxed to the extent that humans are no longer evolving. However, others argue that we are still evolving, because not everyone makes equal contributions to the next generation. In addition, they predict that changing climate and increasing populations will create renewed evolutionary pressures.

How evolution may impact how future humans look is impossible to predict. Ironically, the most significant changes in our looks compared to those early farmers are not genetic at all. Increases in height can be tied to better nutrition, obesity is linked to diet and sedentary lifestyles, and smaller jaws develop when people eat softer-textured food. Although genetic factors play a role in height, metabolism, and bone structure, these changes have taken place too rapidly to be purely genetic.

World tour

What caused the migration of early humans out of Africa? Did sufficient climatic change occur to make it better to leave than to risk trying to adapt to some sort of environmental change?

Based on genetic and fossil evidence, it is widely accepted that humans originated in Africa. Many researchers recognize two major phases of dispersal. The first, Out of Africa 1, began almost 2 million years ago with *Homo erectus*, the first truly upright-walking human ancestor. The second, Out of Africa 2, began about 100,000 years ago with *Homo sapiens*, which evolved in Africa between the two phases of dispersal and eventually replaced archaic humans.

Other researchers consider this view simplistic. They generally agree about the early dispersal, but they propose that multiple later dispersals occurred, some of which may have been from Europe and Asia back to Africa. One reason for the uncertainty is that human fossils are rare compared with stone artifacts, and the cultural traits implied by the tools cannot be reliably tied to biological characteristics of the populations that created them.

What caused humans to disperse is unknown. Some explanations focus on unique features of human culture. Other explanations, acknowledging that other successful species also disperse, focus on environmental changes.

One hypothesis is that the first dispersal was caused by one group of humans outcompeting another. This hypothesis is based on the discovery that two technologically distinct populations of humans existed at the time, and only the population of less advanced toolmakers dispersed from Africa, perhaps because they were at a disadvantage on their shared range. A hypothesis based on advances in toolmaking and competition between groups also has been proposed to explain the second dispersal.

Oscillations from wet to dry conditions occurred around the times of the early and late dispersals. The climatic changes were accompanied by the dispersal of other large animals, which may have been followed and exploited by human populations.

Whatever the reason the dispersals began, a factor that probably facilitated them by enhancing humans' survival is the reduction in zoonotic diseases. These are diseases, such as sleeping sickness, that typically rely on animals for transmission but also affect humans. Zoonotic diseases are especially prevalent in parts of Africa, compared to cooler, drier climates away from the tropics.

Tree house

Why did early man come down from the trees, when he had no protection on the ground from predators such as lions and tigers?

The dominant view among researchers who study human evolution has been that, beginning about 5 million years ago, ground-dwelling humans who could exploit large herds of game on the African savannah arose from tree-dwelling, vegetarian apes. Some maintain that key human traits, including our upright walk and big brains, evolved because of the challenges of life on the open savannah.

Clearly the greater risk of predation and fierce competition for prey are problems with this hypothesis. If it is accurate, the transition from trees to savannah was probably gradual and fueled by climate change. The transition is thought to have taken place at a time when the African continent was becoming more arid, which would have resulted in the fragmentation of forested areas. Hominins—bipedal primates—would have been forced to spend more time on the ground moving between wooded areas and would have needed to exploit resources available in grasslands.

Other researchers make the case that humans could not control large plains until they domesticated riding animals—horses in Asia and camels in more arid regions—and that occurred within the past 10,000 years. Dissatisfaction with the savannah-dwelling hypothesis has recently led to the proposal of two alternatives: the aquarboreal hypothesis and the tectonic hypothesis.

According to the aquarboreal hypothesis, the transition from trees to ground occurred in coastal forests, where hominins could gather wetland plants and shellfish. As forests became more fragmented, hominins later dispersed along coastal areas and rivers. A beachcomber phase that included diving could explain humans' excellent voluntary breath control, subcutaneous fat layer, and lack of fur. Such traits are unique among primates but are found in dolphins, hippos, and walruses.

According to the tectonic hypothesis, hominins evolved and expanded in the African Rift, which extends from north to south along eastern Africa. The rift is a rugged terrain formed by volcanic activity and plate tectonics—movement and deformation of the Earth's crust. Within this complex topography, agile bipeds could gain a tactical advantage over faster-moving quadruped prey and find protection from predators. Humans may have dispersed from Africa into Europe and Asia along a virtually continuous line of tectonically active terrain, as suggested by the locations of the earliest and best-documented sites of human occupation outside of Africa.

Loners

Many different animals, such as birds, have hundreds of different species. Why aren't there tens or hundreds of different species of humans?

In *Bones, Stones and Molecules* (2004), authors David Cameron and Colin Groves comment that researchers who work with the fossil record consider the present era, which has only one *Homo* species, as a unique time in the history of our lineage. In other words, multiple species of humans probably coexisted at various times in human history.

Based on the known fossil data, most scientists propose that archaic humans first dispersed from Africa approximately 1.8 million years ago. Populations settled in different regions and evolved independently.

Modern humans (*Homo sapiens*) probably emerged in Africa between 250,000 and 150,000 years ago. They later dispersed, and by 40,000 years ago, *Homo sapiens* occupied most parts of Africa, Asia, Europe, and Australia. At that time, the Neanderthals (*Homo neanderthalensis*) still occupied parts of Europe and Asia. *Homo erectus* likely still existed in Indonesia (although the fossil evidence is a bit sketchy).

What happened next has been the subject of much speculation. One hypothesis is that modern humans clashed violently with the indigenous human populations they encountered, eventually eliminating them. Another hypothesis is that some interbreeding occurred, and that, for example, we each have a little Neanderthal in us. Finally, it may be that modern humans were simply more successful at competing for the available resources, and the other human species just died out.

The fossil record is not complete enough to tell us what happened to all early humans. The greatest amount of information is known about the extinction of the Neanderthals, 27,000 years ago. Evidence to suggest that *Homo sapiens* engaged in mass genocide of *Homo neanderthalensis* is lacking. Similarly, the available DNA evidence suggests that interbreeding between modern humans and Neanderthals was uncommon—at least, we did not inherit Neanderthal genes.

It is most likely that modern humans drove Neanderthals to extinction by outcompeting them. Modern humans seem to have hunted and gathered over larger areas than the Neanderthals, who tended to remain in the valley systems they had long occupied. Therefore, modern humans were more efficient at exploiting the environment for limited resources. *Homo erectus* also seems to have become extinct at the same time *Homo sapiens* appeared in their region, likely also as a result of competition for limited resources.

Living link?

On the Science Channel, I saw Oliver, the "questionable chimpanzee." I remember seeing him on the news in the past. I was always intrigued with his upright walk, strong manlike shoulders, and wise eyes. I wondered about his relatives. I found out that Oliver had 47 chromosomes, while chimpanzees have 48 chromosomes. Humans have 46 chromosomes. Does that make Oliver a "link" between a chimp and a human?

Starting in the 1970s, Oliver was promoted as a missing link or "humanzee" because of his unusual physical and behavioral traits, as well as the rumor that he had 47 rather than 48 chromosomes. According to reports, his arms and legs were too long, his ears a funny shape, his head too bald, and his face too small for him to be a chimpanzee. He also walked with a locked-knee bipedal (two-legged) gait.

Primatologists who examined Oliver pointed out that chimps vary widely in their physical characteristics. In addition, most of Oliver's teeth were pulled when he was very young to prevent him from biting people. As a result, the muscles in his lower face and temples, and even the bones in his jaws, remained underdeveloped. His training could account for his bipedal gait.

Despite these explanations, doubts about his karyotype—chromosome number and characteristics—remained. An early genetic test attributed to unidentified "American scholars" depicted 47 chromosomes followed by a question mark and was exploited by Oliver's owners to promote him as a missing link.

The karyotype mystery was not solved definitively until 1998, when Oliver was moved to a sanctuary. The results of genetic tests published that year in the *American Journal of Physical Anthropology* showed that Oliver had 48 chromosomes and that his DNA sequence was highly similar to that of the Central African variety of chimpanzee. The researchers narrowed Oliver's probable birthplace to Gabon by comparing Oliver's DNA sequence to DNA sequences from other chimpanzees of known origin.

Even if Oliver had 47 chromosomes, this would not make him a missing link. During the production of egg and sperm cells, a process called meiosis separates chromosome pairs and reduces the number of chromosomes by half so that an offspring gets one chromosome of each pair from each parent. Errors can occur during meiosis and result in offspring with more or fewer than the normal chromosome number. For example, people with Down syndrome, caused by an extra 21st chromosome, and those with Klinefelter's syndrome, caused by an extra X chromosome, have 47 chromosomes.

Tears for fears

Why is it that when you are about to cry, a lump forms in your throat?

Our bodies instinctively interpret negative emotions such as anger, sorrow, and fear as stress. In the face of a stressful situation, our nervous systems switch from "rest-and-digest" mode to "fight-or-flight" mode. This response is a relic from our pre-civilization days, when stress usually was a result of life-threatening situations.

The switch between modes is a function of the autonomic nervous system (ANS). Because its actions are mostly out of our conscious control, the ANS is also referred to as the involuntary nervous system. It is composed of the sympathetic nervous system, which activates the fight-or-flight response, and the parasympathetic nervous system, which controls opposite but complementary actions to promote recuperation and restart regular body maintenance activities.

To prepare the body to confront or run from danger, the sympathetic nervous system stimulates the adrenal glands to produce adrenalin, dilates the pupils, increases heart rate and blood pressure, and diverts blood from the intestines to make it available to the muscles in the limbs. The cessation of digestion can result in the nausea that often accompanies sorrow.

The sympathetic nervous system also increases air intake into the lungs. To allow more air to enter the lungs, the throat must open. The opening is relatively small during normal breathing. In response to the stress that initiates crying, the glottis—the gap between the vocal cords and the associated muscles in the throat—expands as wide as possible.

In contrast, during the act of swallowing, the airway needs to be closed to keep out food and liquids. As food is pushed down the esophagus, the upper portion of the airway is lifted by the muscles at the back of the throat, the glottis constricts, and the epiglottis—the flap of cartilage lying just beneath the base of the tongue—is closed over the glottis.

The sensation of a lump in the throat is a result of the glottis muscles being told to open and close at the same time. In other words, the glottis is caught in a tug-of-war. The feeling is usually relatively short-lived, but some people under stress experience it for weeks or months. The sensation is called globus syndrome or globus hystericus if medical tests rule out injury or disease as a cause.

Blind dreams

Do people who are born blind dream? If so, what do they see in their dreams?

For most people, dreaming is an intensely visual experience. Visual imagery is nearly always present in the dreams of sighted people, and their dreams are usually in color. Auditory sensations occur in more than half of their dreams, but only a small percentage involve taste, smell, and touch.

Blind people who lost their vision after about age 5 continue to have visual imagery in their dreams. They see new friends, places, and things in their dreams, not simply memories they've retained since before they lost their sight. The fact that dreams do not reflect people's current visual impairment reveals that the dreaming brain does not simply reproduce perceptions (albeit in a new narrative), but actually constructs things that have never been experienced while awake.

In contrast to people who lost their sight later in life, people completely blind since birth (congenitally blind) or shortly thereafter lack the rapid eye movements usually associated with dreaming. However, they do dream, and they tend to describe their dreams in the same visual language as a sighted person. When asked to elaborate, it becomes clear that the "pictures" in their heads have been created through prior experience with other senses. In dream reports made by congenitally blind people, more than half of the sensory references are to touch, smell, and taste. The rest of the sensory references are auditory.

In one study, a congenitally blind woman described a dream about sitting at a table in a nice restaurant. She knew she was at a table through kinesthetic sense—the sense mediated by feedback from organs in the muscles and tendons. She knew it was a nice restaurant because she felt the thick carpet and heard the quiet atmosphere. She had an image of the table because she had previously felt tables. Similarly, a congenitally blind woman in another study described being in a room with a device that looked like an ATM. She said she knew what it looked like from prior experience touching the buttons on an ATM.

Studies that have compared the composition, organization, and themes of the dreams of blind people and sighted people have found few differences. Blind people reported more dreams in which they had a misfortune occur during locomotion or transportation, and dreams about their guide dogs, consistent with the notion that there is continuity between dream content and waking experiences.

Hullabaloo

We are all aware of the increase in violence in our society. Is the increasing amount of electronic noise in the atmosphere possibly interfering with brain waves?

About two decades ago, descriptions of a new illness started showing up in the medical literature. It was actually a diverse collection of symptoms: skin problems, dizziness, headaches, fatigue, muscle pain, nausea, problems with concentration and memory, depression, and nervousness.

More people became convinced that their symptoms were being caused by "electromagnetic pollution." They believed that they were affected, while others working under the same conditions were not, because they were particularly susceptible to environmental electromagnetic fields. Hence, the mysterious illness was dubbed "electromagnetic sensitivity syndrome."

Electromagnetic fields are nothing new. Light is a form of electromagnetic radiation, as are the radio waves that bring us our favorite tunes and talk shows and the microwaves that heat up our frozen dinners. However, advancing technologies and rising demand for electricity have steadily increased our exposure to electromagnetic fields.

In response to concerns about the possible health effects of exposure to electromagnetic fields, the World Health Organization (WHO) launched the International EMF Project in 1996 to review studies on the health effects of exposure to these fields.

One concern is the possibility that low-frequency electromagnetic fields could generate currents within the human body. After all, our heartbeat, communication between nerve cells, and the chemical processes that keep our cells alive involve the movement of charged particles. While large electromagnetic fields could stimulate nerves or affect other biological processes, the WHO concludes that the fields we encounter are too small to produce these effects.

An additional concern is that exposure to radiofrequency fields, especially from cell phones, could cause heating of the brain. Even a small amount of heating by radiofrequency fields has been shown to affect brain activity and behavior in animals. However, the majority of scientists consider the fields produced by cell phones too small to heat the brain.

In laboratory studies it has also been difficult to show that the symptoms of electromagnetic sensitivity syndrome have anything to do with exposure to electromagnetic fields. Therefore, our exposure to these fields does not seem to have any significant effects on health or behavior, including violence, but research is ongoing. The WHO acknowledges that if long-term exposure to these fields negatively impacts a small number of people but is harmless to everyone else, the effects would be tricky to detect.

Sentiment sites

What are emotions? Do they reside in specific parts of our brain, or are they the result of our cognitive thinking? Are emotions genetic, or are they learned? Do animals have emotions?

A fully accepted theory of emotion is lacking, but research has provided tantalizing insights. Our experience tells us that emotions have bodily manifestations such as changes in heart rate, irregular breathing, increased or decreased blood flow to the skin or digestive tract, sweating, and trembling. However, it is not quite as simple as saying that because individuals have a certain set of physiological responses, they experience a particular emotion. Cognition also plays an important role.

When provided with an alternative explanation for their physiological responses, people appear to rationalize what they are feeling, rather than automatically experiencing it as an emotion. In one study, people were given an injection of saltwater and either were told that a side effect of the "vitamin shot" was trembling and a pounding heart or were not told anything. The individuals who had been told about the side effect reported experiencing less intense emotions when placed in an anger-provoking or amusing situation.

Several brain regions play a role in our experience of emotions. The hypothalamus controls the autonomic nervous system, which regulates our physiological responses. The amygdala draws our attention to dangers in the environment that might require an emotional response. The hippocampus is involved in learning and memory, including emotional memories. The cortex helps us choose the most appropriate response in an emotional situation.

Babies can express emotions from a very young age, and expressions of emotion are remarkably cross-cultural. In the late 1960s, researchers discovered that members of a tribe in a remote area of Papua New Guinea, who had never been exposed to Western culture, could accurately interpret facial expressions in photographs of Westerners. And Westerners accurately interpreted the expressions of tribe members. Not all aspects of emotional expression are inborn; cultural rules define when such expressions are appropriate. Which situations evoke emotions is also partly learned.

In 1872, Charles Darwin published *The Expression of Emotion in Man and Animals*, in which he suggested that human expressions of emotion evolved from similar expressions in other animals. One recent study found that chimpanzees shown videos of emotional scenes (a veterinarian pursuing chimps, a chimp getting a treat) could correctly choose a photograph of another chimp expressing the emotion that the scene would evoke. Of course, although other animals produce and interpret what appear to be expressions of emotion, we cannot determine if their subjective experience of emotion is the same as ours.

Feeling groovy

I have read that the cause of pleasure is dopamine in the brain. I have also read that serotonin is the feel-good chemical, and runner's high is said to be due to endorphins in the brain. Which is the main cause of pleasure, or do they all interact?

The neurotransmitters dopamine, serotonin, and endorphins are three of several chemical languages known to play a role in feelings of pleasure and well-being. Nerve cells chatter in more than 100 different dialects, and future research will likely implicate more of these in our brains' pleasure conversations.

The discovery of reward circuitry in the brain dates to the 1950s, when researchers made a surprising discovery while investigating the effects of electrical brain stimulation on rats' ability to learn. When electrodes are implanted in a certain region of the brain, rats will press a lever to the point of exhaustion to self-administer electrical stimulation. People given electrical stimulation in the analogous brain region say the experience is intensely pleasurable.

At the core of this reward circuit are nerve cells that originate near the base of the brain, in the ventral tegmental area. They send projections toward the nucleus accumbens, a structure deep beneath the front of the brain. Dopamine is the main neurotransmitter at these connections. Nerve cells using a variety of neurotransmitters connect the reward circuit with brain regions involved in memory and emotion, which influence the reward response.

This system ensures that an organism eats, drinks, and engages in other adaptive behaviors. Addictive drugs hijack it. For example, heroin makes nerve cells churn out more dopamine. Cocaine inhibits the reuptake of dopamine by the nerve cells that release it, preventing dopamine chatter from being quickly silenced.

In depression, a preeminent factor is the reduced activity of nerve cells that communicate using serotonin. Selective serotonin reuptake inhibitors (SSRIs) are the medication of choice for many depressed people.

Unfortunately, the rate of remission with SSRIs is less than 50 percent, and multiple neurotransmitter systems and multiple brain regions have been implicated in depression. Among them are dopamine and the brain's reward circuitry, consistent with one of the many symptoms of depression, anhedonia—the inability to experience pleasure.

Avid runners talk about the euphoric state they get from long-distance running. Often they cannot abstain from running, even when they are injured. The addictive aspect of running appears to be due to the brain's natural opium—endorphins—which, during strenuous exercise, is released into a region of the brain that controls mood.

Mad genius

It seems that many famous artists and writers have suffered from bouts of madness. Is there a relationship between creativity and mental illness, or does it just seem that way because odd or tragic characters are more likely to be remembered?

The idea that madness and creativity are linked goes back to antiquity, but it is not without controversy. Some schools of psychological thought consider creativity to be linked with sound mental health. Today, the prevailing view is that creative genius and some mental disorders are linked, but not necessarily directly.

Three sources of evidence have been mined to determine the relationship between mental disorders and creativity. First, historical data, especially biographies of renowned creators, have been analyzed for indications of symptoms associated with various psychopathologies. Second, psychiatric research has examined the incidence of diagnosed mental disorders and treatment in samples of contemporary creators. Third, psychometric studies—standard personality questionnaires—have compared creative and noncreative individuals.

Conclusions from the three types of studies are consistent. People who are highly creative are more likely to have certain mental disorders, especially depression, than otherwise comparable, less creative individuals. The prevalence and intensity of the symptoms varies among different domains of creativity. For people working in the creative arts, the lifetime prevalence of depression is 50 percent, compared to between 20 and 30 percent for people in business, scientists, and important social figures. Within the creative arts, writers of poetry and fiction and visual artists are most likely to suffer from depression.

Because the defining symptoms of depression include lack of interest and energy and difficulty concentrating, it is paradoxical that depression is associated with creative behavior. Indeed, depression does not appear to be the cause of creative productivity. During a depressive episode, creativity is not enhanced, and mood stabilizers have been found to increase, rather than diminish, productivity.

Instead, studies suggest that a personality trait, self-reflective rumination—conscious, recurring thoughts focused on one's inner feelings—may be the explanation for the paradox. The tendency to ruminate has been shown to increase vulnerability to depression. Rumination has also been shown to enhance creative ability and interest. In other words, depression and creativity happen to be linked because a third factor causes both.

The role of rumination could also explain the lower prevalence of depression among scientific creators versus artistic creators. Original thinking is important in the arts and sciences. In contrast, introspection is less useful for providing ideas that could advance science than it is for providing original content for poetry and other artistic endeavors.

Out of body

I have had three out-of-body experiences. Is there a relationship between the alternate-universe theory and out-of-body, or are they independent of each other?

Despite their New Age mystique and association with certain substances consumed by hippies, out-of-body experiences are reported by many people, particularly those who suffer from migraines and neurological conditions. Studies of out-of-body experiences have recently been published in highly respected journals, including *Science* and *Nature*.

These studies do not tie the phenomenon to alternate universes, though. The existence of multiple, parallel universes is predicted by the complicated mathematics of quantum physics. Even if these alternate universes exist, physicists say it is impossible to access or even perceive them.

Instead, the study of out-of-body experiences is the purview of psychologists and neuroscientists. Out-of-body experiences have been accidentally induced in patients undergoing focused electrical stimulation of the brain during epilepsy treatment. For example, one patient described an instantaneous feeling of lightness and the sensation that she was floating above the bed during the electrical stimulation of a region of her brain called the angular gyrus.

The angular gyrus is on the surface of the brain, toward the rear, and it is a region that receives input about vision, hearing, and touch. The angular gyrus is also close to the vestibular cortex, which processes sensory information to maintain the sense of balance. The brain stimulation research suggests that out-of-body experiences may be caused by the dissociation of information coming simultaneously from two or more senses.

This hypothesis is supported by recent studies that used head-mounted video displays to give people visual information that placed them in a different location. The visual information on its own did not give people the feeling of being outside their bodies. But when they saw their virtual body being touched at the same time as their real body was being touched, they felt as if the virtual body was their own body. Then, when a hammer was swung so that it appeared to hit the virtual body, measurements of skin conductance—a measurement of stress—indicated that the hammer was registered as a threat, even though it posed no real danger.

The studies show that information from the senses can modify the brain's representation of the physical body. In addition to shedding light on out-of body experiences, the research provides insight into consciousness, since the feeling of being within one's physical body is a foundation of the concept of self.

Musical mind

Your out-of-body experience answer must have been reassuring to anyone who's had the experience and was disbelieved when they described the event. I'm writing about a different kind of "out-of-body" experience—music playing in one's head. In addition to a variety of music, I also hear noisy motors, a distant train, or nonmusical drumming. Have you come across any information on this kind of auditory hallucination?

Everyone has had an earworm—a snippet of a song playing repeatedly in their head like a broken record. Someone's ringtone, a visit to Disneyland, or even the mere mention of an annoying tune (I promise I'll refrain) is enough to set it off. What distinguishes a musical hallucination from an earworm is that a musical hallucination appears to originate from outside your head.

People are often afraid to admit that they are hearing things for fear they will be thought of as mentally ill. But auditory hallucinations seem to be fairly common in mentally sound people who have ear problems. In one study, researchers interviewed 32 people who had lost hearing in both ears and discovered that all had experienced musical hallucinations.

These hallucinations are a form of tinnitus—usually a more generic buzzing or ringing in the ears. Changes in fluid levels in the inner ear (with or without hearing loss), as occur in Ménière's disease, can cause auditory hallucinations in some people, as can many drugs, including alcohol, blood pressure medication, and even aspirin.

Musical hallucinations are considered to be analogous to Charles Bonnet syndrome, in which visually impaired people see things that are not there, and phantom limb syndrome, in which amputees have sensations that seem to be in their missing limb. The common link among these syndromes is sensory deprivation. According to one explanation (Release Theory), normal sensory input suppresses the nerve circuits in which sensory memories are stored. When these circuits are no longer inhibited, previously recorded perceptions are "released" and re-experienced.

Depending on the cause, musical hallucinations can be reduced with a hearing aid (if hearing loss is involved), controlling the body's retention of fluids (if changes in fluid volume in the inner ear are involved), or changing medications in consultation with a physician. One case report described a woman who could "think" down the volume of her musical hallucinations.

Perhaps it is even possible to harness the hallucinations for good. Some researchers believe that musicians are predisposed to musical hallucinations. Famous composers, including Beethoven and Schumann, experienced them.

8

Health nuts

Counting calories

How do nutritionists determine the caloric content of a complex dish when it is impossible or impractical to total up the individual ingredients?

One way is to measure the amount of thermal energy produced when the food is completely combusted into carbon dioxide and water in a device called a bomb calorimeter. To avoid overestimating the actual calories available from food, bomb calorimetry measurements of fecal matter must be subtracted from those of the food.

This method is sometimes used for animal feed, but it is not very popular because bomb calorimeters are pricy. Plus, it is kind of a drag for researchers to have to follow people around with baggies to determine the caloric content of what passes through our digestive systems unscathed.

Instead, total energy content is usually determined by adding up the energy contributions of fat, proteins, and carbohydrates in food. Fat can be extracted from the food with chemical solvents and then quantified. Protein contains 16 percent nitrogen on average, so the amount of protein is calculated from food's total nitrogen content. The amount of carbohydrate is usually calculated from the total mass of the food minus the amount of fat, protein, moisture, and minerals.

Back in the late 19th century, W. O. Atwater and other researchers at the U.S. Department of Agriculture did the dirty work to determine the average amount of energy yielded from fat, protein, and carbohydrates after accounting for losses in digestion. The conversion factors are 9 calories (referred to as kilocalories outside the United States) per gram of fat, 4 calories per gram of protein, and 4 calories per gram of carbohydrate.

The 9-4-4 conversion factors can be misleading because different fats, proteins, and carbohydrates have different structures and digestibilities. For example, multiplying the total grams of carbohydrate by 4 overestimates the amount of energy the body can extract from high-fiber foods. For this reason, the mass of insoluble fiber usually is subtracted from the total carbohydrate before the energy calculation is made.

If the exact ingredients are known, it is possible to use the Atwater specific factor system, which is a series of tables listing the number of calories in the fats, carbohydrates, and proteins in specific foods. For example, the tables reveal that the protein in eggs provides nearly 1 more calorie per gram than the protein in soybeans. On average, the specific factor system yields energy values that are about 5 percent lower than those obtained using the general conversion factors.

Fat carbs, skinny carbs

What's the big deal about carbohydrates? Why should we be on a low-carb diet? (Or should we?)

You are right to be skeptical. We are at one end of a pendulum swing. Remember not so long ago, when fat was the bad guy and "low-fat" or "no-fat" labels sold food?

Throughout much of the low-fat era, we acted as if as long as we ate foods that were low in fat, we could eat whatever we wanted, even if the foods were high in calories or sugar. The problem is simple: if you take in more calories than you burn, regardless of whether those calories are from fat or carbohydrates, you gain weight.

Cutting carbohydrates results in weight loss only if total calorie intake is reduced, not if the calories from carbohydrates are simply replaced by calories from fat or protein.

Toward the end of the low-fat era, but before the low-carb craze, we started to develop a more nuanced view of fat, accepting, for example, that fish oils can help reduce heart disease. Now we also need to develop a less black-and-white view of carbohydrates.

Not all carbs are created equal. Many of the carbohydrates in the typical American diet come from highly refined grains. To make them easier to use in cooking, grains are milled to remove their outer coating, leaving the starchy portion of the grain. Unfortunately, the outer portion of the grain is high in fiber, B vitamins, and trace minerals such as copper and zinc.

In addition, foods made from refined grains, like white bread, are digested quickly into glucose, causing blood sugar to spike rapidly. Foods that cause rapid increases in blood sugar are said to have a high glycemic index, and diets that are filled with such foods have been linked to heart disease and diabetes.

On the other hand, carbohydrates like brown bread, brown rice, and whole grain pasta have a low glycemic index. Not only do they not cause spikes in blood sugar, but they also are rich in vitamins, minerals, and fiber, which can protect against cancer and decrease cholesterol.

Most Americans do not get enough servings of whole gains every day. You can find out more about carbohydrates and the glycemic index at the Harvard School of Public Health website: http://www.hsph.harvard.edu/nutritionsource/carbohydrates.html.

Perhaps in terms of diet we could learn from the French, who are inclined to define healthy eating more in terms of balance, variety, and freshness. Healthy eating is not about demonizing certain foods. Studies repeatedly show that Americans are not getting enough of the foods that are good for us, especially fruits, vegetables, and whole grains. Hopefully, when the pendulum swings again, "balance" will be the *mot du jour*.

Combo meal

For breakfast, I usually have orange juice, an egg, toast, and coffee. If I ate these items separately over a period of, say, two to three hours, would I get more nutritional benefit from this combination of food, rather than by eating them all in one sitting?

Despite our natural aversion to pairing certain foods (pickle cookies, anyone?) and the popularity of "dissociated diets," there is limited scientific data on the value of eating foods separately versus in combination.

It is well known that vitamins and minerals can interact synergistically or antagonistically, but most of these interactions are determined by the composition of the overall diet. For example, a magnesium deficiency can interfere with the body's metabolism of sodium, potassium, calcium, and phosphorus.

Within a single meal, some nutrient interactions occur. One study showed that when calcium was added to a meal, it significantly reduced iron absorption. So calcium fortification of orange juice or milk in your coffee could reduce the amount of iron your body can extract from your toast and egg. On the other hand, the vitamin C in orange juice facilitates iron absorption. In any case, the body seems to adjust over time, because another study showed that iron levels in the blood were unaffected by taking calcium supplements with two meals daily for a few months.

Proponents of dissociated diets would tell you to eat your egg separately from your toast and juice, and not to add butter or whole milk to your breakfast mix, because intake of carbohydrates, fats, and proteins should be spread throughout the day. One of their arguments is that if carbohydrates, which effectively simulate the release of insulin, are ingested with fats, insulin will cause more fat to be stored.

This argument was debunked in a comparison of two low-calorie diets—one that combined fats and carbohydrates within meals, and another that separated fats and carbohydrates into different meals. Weight loss was the same in the group on the dissociated diet as it was for the group on the mixed diet. Both diets decreased blood glucose, insulin, cholesterol, and blood pressure by a similar amount.

Some people recommend minimizing the intake of liquids with food to avoid diluting the digestive enzymes, but if your goal is to rehydrate, this rule doesn't hold water. Liquids are better retained when they are consumed with meals.

Of course, individual foods are a combination of many nutrients. For instance, an egg is approximately equal parts protein and fat, with a tad of carbohydrate and a long list of vitamins and minerals. So our digestive systems come equipped to tackle those pickle cookies—if only our palates were up to it.

Chug-a-lug

I try to drink eight glasses of water a day, but instead of drinking one glass every hour or so, I drink three 8-ounce glasses when I wake up in the morning, another three at lunch, and two in the afternoon. Am I getting the necessary hydration that my body needs?

Aliens studying earthlings over the past couple decades would almost certainly have noted a strange phenomenon: we have become as attached to our water bottles as Charlie Brown's friend Linus is attached to his blanket. (I confess: A large water bottle is within reach as I write this.)

"'Drink at least eight glasses of water a day.' Really? Is there scientific evidence for '8x8'?" may seem like a surprising title for a journal article (published in the *American Journal of Physiology* in 2002) considering the ubiquitous nature of this health recommendation. Perhaps even more surprising is the conclusion of its author, Heinz Valtin, a physician and kidney specialist at Dartmouth Medical School.

Although Valtin found some evidence that individuals with very low fluid intake are at greater risk for bladder cancer, colorectal cancer, heart disease, and migraines, the research studies failed to definitively prove the connection. Overall, he concluded that the wide range of claims about the health benefits of drinking eight glasses of water a day is largely unsupported. He also argued that although hot weather and physical activity increase water needs, eight glasses is more than sedentary individuals in a temperate climate typically need.

In terms of getting the maximum hydration from the water consumed, a study found that a few glasses of water ingested over a couple of hours are largely retained, while the same amount of water ingested in 15 minutes is not. Individual variation is large and depends on daily salt intake. The sodium ion concentration in the blood influences a brain sensor called an osmostat, which sends signals that control thirst and water retention.

Water ingested with food is better retained, and contrary to popular belief, it does not slow digestion. Rats allowed to drink during a meal digested their food at the same rate as rats deprived of water during the meal.

Water intake can influence calorie intake. On a 12-week diet, middle-aged and older adults who drank two glasses of water a half hour before meals ate less and lost 5 pounds more than those who did not drink water before meals. Water does not seem to curb appetite in younger adults, but in another study, increasing the water content of the foods themselves decreased calorie intake.

Cocoa craze

Is chocolate good for you? Does it matter what kind of chocolate you eat?

Chocolate has been touted as "the new red wine" for its putative health benefits. The excitement centers on a class of compounds called flavonoids, which are antioxidants. Raw cocoa is one of the richest known sources of flavonoids, with more than 10 percent flavonoids by weight.

Studies indicate that isolated flavonoids, or chocolate that contains flavonoids, may have favorable effects on five risk factors associated with heart disease. First, flavonoids scavenge free radicals, thereby inhibiting the oxidation of low-density lipoprotein (LDL). This process is beneficial because the oxidation of LDL promotes the formation of plaques—deposits—in the arteries. Second, flavonoids inhibit another early event in plaque formation—the adherence of white blood cells to the lining of the arteries.

Third, they increase high-density lipoprotein (HDL), which helps remove cholesterol from the body. Fourth, like aspirin, flavonoids reduce the reactivity of platelets—the smallest structural units in the blood. As a result, platelets become less likely to stick together to form a blood clot. Fifth, flavonoids increase nitric oxide levels, which dilates the blood vessels and reduces blood pressure.

Some evidence suggests that flavonoids protect against cancer and possibly neurodegenerative diseases. They have also been shown to decrease insulin resistance.

However, all the support for the health benefits of flavonoids comes from epidemiological studies and very short-term experimental studies. Although epidemiological studies address the long-term consumption of flavonoids, such studies are problematic because they compare naturally occurring populations, which may differ in more than just their cocoa consumption habits. So far, no long-term experimental studies have addressed the health benefits of chocolate consumption, nor have different types of chocolate been systematically compared.

Not all chocolate is created equal. The concentration of flavonoids depends on the variety of cocoa plant and the growing conditions. By far the most important factor in flavonoid concentration is how the beans were processed. Most chocolate products on the market today contain little or no flavonoids because flavonoids are destroyed by fermentation, roasting, and treatment with alkali. Experimental studies of chocolate consumption often use non-commercially available high-flavonoid chocolate.

If otherwise processed the same way, dark chocolate contains more flavonoids than milk chocolate. In the United States, the Food and Drug Administration mandates that dark chocolate contain at least 15 percent chocolate liquor from ground or melted cocoa nibs. Milk chocolate must contain at least 10 percent. White chocolate does not contain any cocoa solids and therefore is devoid of flavonoids.

Go the distance

There has been speculation that women will do better than men in ultra marathons of 50 miles, 100 miles, or more, because male marathon runners "hit the wall" after about 20 miles, when they've used almost all their glycogen and start burning mostly fat. Women don't have this problem, because they are better at burning fat. Is there much evidence that women are doing better than men in ultra marathons?

Until 1972, women were officially barred from running marathons in the United States, and not until 1984 were they permitted to run the Olympic marathon. Once women were allowed to compete in the 26.2-mile race, their times improved so rapidly that a 1992 article in the journal *Nature* predicted that women would catch up to men by 1998. That did not happen, but now less than 12 minutes separate the fastest female and male marathoners.

In the ultra (anything longer than a marathon), women have already caught up to men—at least in one race. In 2002 and 2003 a female runner won one of the world's most grueling races, the Badwater Ultramarathon. The race begins in the Badwater Basin in Death Valley, California, and continues 135 miles to the base of Mount Whitney, with more than 8,500 feet of elevation gain, in brutal summer heat. Women are often in the top five finishers of Badwater.

Many hypotheses have been proposed to explain why women may have an advantage over men in long-distance running. Psychological factors, such as better resistance to pain or better ability to pace oneself, could play a role. Size may matter; lighter runners are better able to maintain a balance between production and dissipation of thermal energy. Some studies, but not all, have found that women burn fat better than men do during prolonged exercise.

After years of dramatic improvements, female distance runners now seem to be improving at the same rate, rather than faster than men. Also, men and women who ran equally fast at near-marathon distance performed similarly in 50-mile and 100-mile races, in the largest comparison to date. So the idea that women have an advantage over men at long distances is still controversial.

Marathons, even ultras, have become a social and fitness phenomenon. More than 400,000 marathon finishing times were recorded in the United States last year, and women are now 40 percent of marathon finishers. Considering how recently women's distance running gained societal acceptance, I think we ain't seen nothin' yet!

Exercise regimen

I try to run four miles a day on my treadmill, but I don't have the stamina to do it all at one time. Therefore, I run one mile, and later I run another mile, and so on. Is there a drawback to the benefits I receive by breaking it up this way (such as calories burned)?

Many studies have compared the benefits of continuous versus split exercise sessions because any differences have implications for public health recommendations. This research suggests that the health benefits of split exercise sessions compare favorably with those of continuous exercise sessions.

Regardless of the structure of the workout, the number of calories burned is elevated both during and after exercise. This means that the same old couch potato routine burns more calories after a workout. How long your metabolism remains cranked up after exercise depends on the workout's duration and intensity. The increase in metabolism following exercise is due to the many processes involved in repairing and getting fuel back into the muscles, and removing lactic acid and other cellular waste products.

Splitting the same workout into multiple sessions does not alter how many calories are burned during the total workout, as long as the total work performed remains the same. But some studies show that the post-exercise calorie burn is greater when the workout session is split. The difference is small—it would amount to about one slice of apple pie guilt-free after a month of daily split workouts instead of continuous workouts. Varying the intensity during a continuous workout, while maintaining the same average intensity, has been shown to have the same effect as splitting the workout.

Split and continuous workouts also seem to have an equally favorable effect on blood pressure, other measures of cardiorespiratory fitness, and cholesterol levels. The only caveat is that nearly all the studies comparing continuous and split workouts have been short-term. Therefore, it is possible that undiscovered long-term differences exist in how different workout schedules affect the risk of heart disease, diabetes, and cancer.

The 2008 Physical Activity Guidelines for Americans from the U.S. Department of Health and Human Services (http://www.health.gov/paguidelines/) recommend that adults get at least 2.5 hours, and preferably at least 5 hours, of moderately intense physical activity each week. Anything that gets you moving is fair game, but a combination of muscle-strengthening and aerobic exercise is ideal. According to the guidelines, episodes of aerobic activity should be at least 10 minutes long.

Pounding the pavement

When walking/jogging through our suburban neighborhood, I stay on the sidewalk for safety. My wife claims that walking/jogging in the street is easier on the joints, because it is a "softer" surface. Assuming that she is not hit by a car first, is there really any difference to an average recreational jogger/walker between concrete and blacktop?

According to conventional wisdom, concrete is a more damaging running surface than asphalt. A runner strikes the ground approximately 1,000 times per mile. Therefore, anything that reduces the impact of each foot strike, even by a small amount, should decrease stress-related injuries.

In May 1997, *Runner's World* magazine rated running surfaces from worst (1) to best (10). Here are surfaces and their ratings: snow (2), concrete (2.5), sand (6), asphalt (6), treadmill (6.5), synthetic track (7), cinders (7.5), dirt (8), wood chips (9), and grass (9.5).

Some articles in popular magazines cite clinical studies that claim improper running surface is a leading cause of stress-related injuries. However, studies of injured runners visiting clinics cannot prove that running on a particular surface caused an injury. It is also necessary to determine how many people run on that surface without pulling up lame.

A search turned up four studies in the medical literature that compared injuries in people who ran primarily on concrete versus those who ran primarily on asphalt. In total, more than 4,600 recreational and competitive runners were surveyed and resurveyed over a period of 2 to 12 months. Three of the studies found that running surface made no difference in the number of injuries sustained.

The fourth study found that running surface made no difference in injuries to male runners, but that female runners who ran on concrete more than two-thirds of the time had more injuries than those who ran primarily on asphalt. This was the smallest of the four studies, and it had only 15 female runners who ran primarily on concrete. It is possible that something else about these runners predisposed them to injury.

An interesting biomechanics study, published in *Sports Medicine* in October 1986, may help explain why runners' injuries do not seem to be related to surface hardness. The study's author found, unexpectedly, that the peak value of the vertical force caused by a foot striking concrete was actually lower than on asphalt or grass. The runner's foot also remained in contact with the concrete a few milliseconds longer than with the other surfaces.

This led to the conclusion that just before striking the surface, the runner subconsciously adjusts leg stiffness based on perception of surface hardness to cushion the landing.

Totally radical

I understand that antioxidants decrease the number of free radicals in the body. How do you determine your number of free radicals?

Free radicals (the kind generated in chemical reactions, not in Berkeley in the '60s) are molecules with unpaired electrons. Electrons like to hang out in pairs, and when they find themselves solitary, they try to break up happy electron couples in other molecules.

DNA, proteins, and fats can all be damaged by free radicals, and free radicals have been implicated in a wide range of diseases, including cancer, Alzheimer's disease, and heart disease.

Free radicals' bad rap is not entirely fair, however. They are produced as a normal part of many chemical reactions in our cells, and they play a number of important roles in the body. For example, our immune system uses free radicals as weapons against invading bacteria and viruses.

It is not possible to find out how many free radicals you have. Doctors don't test for free radicals because the complexity of different body tissues makes these tests impractical, according to Joseph Scherger, a professor and physician at the University of California San Diego School of Medicine.

Scherger points out that although elevated levels of free radicals cannot be measured directly, their effects can be measured. For example, free radicals can cause inflammation in the blood vessels, which leads to atherosclerosis, or clogging of the arteries. Inflammation increases the amount of a chemical in the blood called C-reactive protein (CRP). So levels of CRP provide indirect information about free radical activity.

Someday, it might be possible to scan for free radical activity in particular organs or tissues. Electron spin resonance—a measurement technique that detects free radicals based on how they behave in a magnetic field—has been used to detect free radicals in small animals. Several challenges to extending this technique to humans exist. For instance, it involves administering chemicals that are unsafe to humans to trap the radicals so that they can be measured.

It might be difficult to draw conclusions from a free radical test, since levels of free radicals are dynamic. Elevated free radicals might be a sign of a chronic problem or your body's normal response to a temporary infection.

So even with such a test, advice from doctors on how to keep a balance between free radicals and antioxidants would still be to avoid smoking, minimize intake of trans fats, and keep your diet rich in fruits and vegetables.

It's elemental

What can you tell me about indium—element 49—and its role, if any, in human nutrition? Are there any websites I can look at?

An Internet search turns up some amazing claims about the health benefits of indium. Among the plethora of ailments indium is purported to cure are addictions, hair loss, the appearance of aging, cancer, birth defects, low and high blood pressure, and weight problems. Most of these claims are presented without any supporting evidence, but a few sites refer to—but distort—scientific studies.

For example, one site claims that in 1971, Dr. Henry Schroeder discovered that indium supplements resulted in a lower body weight, especially in females, and may give women the extra boost to burn more calories and lose weight. Schroeder published a paper that year, in *The Journal of Nutrition*, describing the effects of low doses of indium (as indium chloride) on the growth and life span of mice. However, he reported that indium stunted the growth of mice, especially females, not that it turned them into fat-burning machines.

Also, in contrast to what one would expect if indium really were a cure-all, Schroeder found no statistically significant differences in the life spans, or numbers of tumors, in mice getting indium supplements compared to controls.

A radioactive isotope of indium is used in medicine, including in cancer treatment, but these uses exploit the radioactivity of the particular isotope, not indium's purported nutritional value.

An increase in the use of indium (nonradioactive, of course) in the electronics industry (for example, in semiconductors and solar cells), and concerns over possible health risks to workers, have stimulated a few recent studies on indium exposure. Animal studies have shown that, in high doses, indium can have adverse effects on the liver and kidneys and on fetal development.

Because many essential minerals are toxic in large doses, the adverse effects of high doses of indium do not disprove the benefits of low doses. However, indium has no known biological function, and the scientific literature does not support the claims about indium's benefits on health.

Color me young

I have heard that middle-aged people can prevent their hair from turning gray by taking a vitamin B complex containing para-amino benzoic acid (PABA). Is there any truth to this?

PABA probably is most familiar as an ingredient once widely used in sunscreens, but bacteria in our intestines also make it. Although PABA is sometimes called vitamin B_x and is found in foods such as brewer's yeast, liver, and whole grains along with other B vitamins, it is not officially classified as a vitamin because its intake is not essential for human health.

The claim that PABA can prevent graying of hair has roots in studies conducted in the 1940s and '50s. They concluded that PABA consumed in large doses caused darkening of hair in some people with white or gray hair. The length of time the hair was gray before PABA treatment began did not appear to influence the darkening effect. One study also noted a darkening of hair in individuals with nongray hair.

The dosages of PABA used in the studies were high, from hundreds to thousands of milligrams per day. Much lower doses (30 milligrams or more) can cause nausea, fever, rashes, and liver toxicity, according to the 2007 edition of *Dietary Supplements*, by pharmacist and nutritionist Pamela Mason.

In addition, the outcomes of the PABA studies were highly variable. In some, the majority of people taking PABA did not have a change in hair color. It is not clear what factors may have led to the inconsistent results, or even how PABA could reverse graying.

Severe malnutrition can cause graying of hair, as can large deficiencies of individual nutrients, including copper, zinc, and folic acid. Nonetheless, genetics appears to be the dominant factor that determines when an individual's hair turns gray.

Hair color depends on the presence or absence of the pigment melanin, which is produced in organelles called melanosomes within cells called melanocytes by the process of (don't worry, tedium does not cause gray hair) melanogenesis.

Gray hair has a marked reduction in the number of active melanocytes within the hair bulb. As a result, fewer melanosomes are incorporated into the growing hair shaft.

The pigment changes are accompanied by alterations in the hair structure as the central, or medullary, layer of the hair thickens and the surrounding cortical layer thins. What triggers the decrease in melanogenesis, and how the pigment changes relate to the changes in the structure and texture of gray hair, are not yet understood.

Vitamin virtues

Does any scientific evidence show whether purchased vitamins (multi- or individual) are effective?

For people with special nutritional needs or vitamin deficiencies, vitamin supplements can be beneficial. An example is supplementation with folic acid before and during pregnancy, which significantly reduces various birth defects, especially spinal deformities.

Even in developed nations, severe vitamin deficiencies are not entirely a thing of the past. Cases of rickets—slowed growth and bone deformities caused by vitamin D deficiency—crop up regularly in small numbers of infants in the United States. Vitamin deficiencies are also common in people over age 65.

More than one-third of U.S. adults take multivitamins, and nearly three-quarters use nutritional supplements of some kind. After multivitamins, the most popular nutritional supplements are calcium, vitamin E, and vitamin C.

Yet, although many studies have examined the effectiveness of multivitamins and individual nutritional supplements on preventing a range of ailments, including cancer, cardiovascular disease, and age-related cognitive declines, results are highly variable. Some show increased risk, others show decreased risk, and still others reveal no effect.

Several comprehensive reviews have concluded that the overall quantity, quality, and consistency of evidence is weak that nutritional supplements benefit the general adult U.S. population. They also call for future research to better control for prior nutritional status of study participants. Furthermore, supplementation studies lasting a few months, or even years, may be inadequate, because chronic diseases can take more than a decade to develop.

Food and Drug Administration oversight of nutritional supplements is loose. Supplements are categorized as food rather than as drugs, which have tighter oversight, and supplements sometimes contain contaminants. For instance, a study by the International Olympic Committee showed that some supplements for athletes contained undeclared steroids.

Products that have the ConsumerLab.com "CL Seal" have been tested for product label accuracy and ingredient quality. Similarly, the verification mark of US Pharmacopeia (USP), a nonprofit, nongovernment organization, signifies that the supplement was produced through USP-verified good manufacturing practices.

The FDA is phasing in new regulations that require manufacturers to evaluate the composition of their supplements. However, none of these oversights ensures that the product works. Without FDA review, labels are allowed to claim that a supplement affects a body structure or function (but not that it prevents or treats disease).

Fuel economy

What is a person's metabolic rate based on?

Metabolic rate has three components: resting metabolic rate (the energy it takes just to be alive—to breathe and for our cells to go about their daily business), the energy expended on eating (digesting, absorbing, and storing food), and the energy required for all other activities.

Resting metabolic rate accounts for approximately 60 percent of the calories we expend every day. Eating (excluding the calories burned getting to the nearest burger joint) makes up about 10 percent of daily energy expenditure. The remaining 30 percent of calories are burned as a result of activity.

Activity can be divided into exercise and nonexercise activity thermogenesis (NEAT). NEAT is the energy burned during daily activities that are not fitness-related, such as standing, ambulating, and fidgeting. Researchers discovered, by having people wear motion-sensing undergarments, that lean, self-proclaimed "couch potatoes" engage in approximately two hours more NEAT behaviors each day than their obese counterparts. The differences in NEAT meant that the obese people burned 350 fewer calories per day than the lean people. Interestingly, even when the obese people lost weight, they did not increase their NEAT.

In fact, another study showed that even moderate weight loss (15 to 20 pounds, or 7 to 9 kilograms) actually decreases metabolic rate. This finding explains why it is difficult to maintain weight loss through dieting alone: the body burns fewer calories at the new, lower weight. On the other hand, exercise burns calories in the short term and can crank up metabolic rate in the long term by building muscle.

Muscle mass determines a large proportion of the individual differences in metabolic rate, because, even at rest, muscle tissue consumes more fuel than fat. Differences in muscle mass explain why women have, on average, a 10 percent lower total daily energy expenditure than men. Also, metabolism tends to slow down with age because of loss of muscle mass, not just because of reduced activity.

Metabolism is regulated by intricate feedback mechanisms between the body and the brain. For example, during starvation, certain thyroid hormones drop rapidly, leading to a 40 percent decrease in resting metabolic rate. The thyroid gland is under the influence of the pituitary gland in the brain, which receives orders from a brain region known as the hypothalamus. The hypothalamus is influenced by leptin, which is produced by fat cells. When it was discovered a decade ago, leptin (from the Greek *leptos*, meaning thin) was thought to have potential as a magic skinny pill, but alas, controlling metabolism is not so simple.

Fit to be sweaty

I read somewhere that people who are aerobically fit sweat more than people who are less fit. Is this true?

Studies have shown that people who are aerobically fit do sweat more, and begin sweating more quickly, than people who are less fit when they exercise at similar *relative* intensities.

"Relative intensity" means a fixed percentage—say, 80 percent—of individuals' maximal aerobic power, which is ascertained from a person's oxygen uptake and carbon dioxide production during exercise. To get a fit person to exercise at 80 percent of his or her maximal aerobic power, experimenters need to crank up the tension on an exercise bicycle, or the incline or speed of a treadmill, compared to the setting that gets a nonfit person exercising at 80 percent of maximal power.

Exercise physiologists compare people who are exercising at the same relative intensity, rather than doing an identical task, because they are trying to understand how the body adapts to training, and what happens to sweating, heart rate, oxygen consumption, and so on as people get close to their physical limits, whatever those limits are.

Therefore, a couch potato probably would sweat more than a marathoner when trotting 100 feet to the mailbox. But fit people get more sweaty, more quickly when they push themselves equally hard with respect to their own physical limits. Other individual differences, including gender (on average, men sweat more than women), also influence sweating.

Red and white

My daughter does not eat red meat. I've seen the TV commercial from the pork industry that calls pork "the other white meat," suggesting that it compares to chicken as far as nutrition is concerned. How does pork compare to beef?

This advertisement is a clever marketing ploy by the pork industry, which is attempting to piggyback on the growing popularity of chicken. Since the 1970s, per-capita consumption of chicken has increased, while consumption of beef has declined. Pork consumption has held relatively steady, at 50 pounds per person annually.

Although pork is paler than beef, the U.S. Department of Agriculture classifies all meat from livestock—including pork, veal, beef, and lamb—as red meat. The red color comes from myoglobin, which is an iron-containing protein that holds oxygen in muscle. Pork has less myoglobin than beef, but more than the white meat of chicken.

Hogs are leaner than they used to be due to improved breeding and feeding, but clearly fat content and nutritional value also depend on the cut of pork selected and how it is cooked. Studies have shown that cholesterol and triglyceride levels in consumers of lean pork, lean beef, or white meat (chicken or fish) following a fat-controlled diet are similar. This indicates that these levels depend on the fat content, not the protein source itself.

Meat is a good source of minerals and B vitamins. On average, pork has less iron and zinc than beef, but about the same amount of copper. In terms of the B vitamins, pork has more thiamine than beef and about the same amount of niacin and riboflavin.

Your daughter may be concerned about fat intake, or studies that have linked consumption of red meat to increased risk of certain types of cancer, including colon and breast cancer. The exact relationship between red meat consumption and cancer risk is uncertain because consumers of red meat and nonconsumers usually have other differences in diet. For instance, people who abstain from eating red meat may consume more fruits and vegetables high in antioxidants.

People avoid certain types of meat for a variety of reasons besides health concerns. Certain animals may be labeled sacred or unclean by their religion. They may feel that it is unethical to eat mammals or any animal. They may also be concerned about the environmental impact of factory farms, or that more resources are needed to produce meat than an equal amount of calories from a plant source.

Hold the sunny side

Since the medical profession touts the need to avoid excess egg consumption due to the yolks, I've been wondering why science has not made any effort to create a smaller yolk content. Or has this been attempted?

Chickens lay the occasional yolkless egg, but hens that consistently produce meringue-ready eggs would be expensive and technically difficult to breed. After all, the yolk is not just a critical ingredient in hollandaise sauce, but it also provides nourishment for a developing chick. So eggs with no yolk, or a very small yolk, would be sterile.

Each egg starts out as a single cell in the ovary of the mother's body. The egg cells are already present when a female bird hatches. When she is a few months old, yolk is added to one of these cells. A surge in estrogen stimulates the liver to produce vitellogenin, the major protein in egg yolk. Vitellogenin is transported to the oviduct—the tube that leads from the ovary—via the bloodstream.

The finished yolk passes down the oviduct to the place where the albumen, or egg white, is produced. The albumen is added in layers, and the yolk ends up floating in a watery layer of albumen surrounded by a thick, tough layer of albumen that acts as a shock absorber. The motion of the egg twists the albumen at either end, producing the white string-like anchors—chalazae—that keep the yolk centered.

If everything is functioning normally, the outer membrane and shell are added further down the oviduct, and the hen lays a perfect egg. When things go awry, eggs can end up with double yolks or no yolks. The oviduct is an assembly line with multiple eggs in progress at once. If two yolks drop into the oviduct at the same time, they may end up encased in the same albumen and shell. Conversely, if something interferes with yolk production, the hen may lay an egg containing albumen only.

The size of the yolk relative to the albumen increases as hens age. Also, across different breeds of chickens, a moderate amount of natural variation occurs in the ratio of yolk to albumen. Theoretically, yolks could be made even smaller by tinkering with one or more of the at least four genes involved in vitellogenin production.

Egg yolks have gotten a bad rap because of their cholesterol content, but the yolk has a richer concentration of vitamins and minerals than the white. Studies have shown that eating an egg or two a day does not increase heart disease risk in healthy individuals.

Grain of salt

Recently, some TV commercials have claimed that their products contain "sea salt that contains less sodium than regular table salt." Aren't they both sodium chloride (NaCl)? And don't we get some of our table salt from seawater? Also, it has become very difficult to avoid excess salt. Some products contain more than 1,000 mg of sodium per serving. Is there any way to get these manufacturers to use a lot less salt?

For people competing in endurance events, hyponatremia—an abnormally low concentration of sodium in the blood—is a real danger when they drink too much water without replenishing the sodium lost in sweat. However, in most countries the average salt (sodium chloride) intake is at least double the maximum 5 grams (about one teaspoonful, or 2,300 milligrams of sodium) per day recommended by the World Health Organization.

Multiple sources of evidence show that high salt consumption can increase blood pressure. Elevated blood pressure is the single most important cause of heart attack and stroke. However, studies reveal considerable individual variation in the effect of salt consumption on blood pressure.

Salty foods irritate the stomach lining, and high consumption has been linked to stomach cancer. Some evidence also suggests that high salt intake can lead to water retention, increase the risk of kidney stones, contribute to osteoporosis, and worsen asthma symptoms.

Over 85 percent of the mineral composition of seawater is sodium chloride. The purer the sea salt, the more sodium chloride it contains. The label on my inexpensive bottle of sea salt says that it is more than 99 percent sodium chloride. That is about the same as regular table salt, which is mostly mined from deposits left by ancient salt lakes. Low-sodium salt is sodium chloride mixed with another mineral salt, such as potassium chloride.

Most dietary salt comes from processed food, so check the sodium content on the label, because the manufacturer's claims may be misleading. Salt has been used as a preservative for thousands of years and has other roles in cooking, but it is often added to make poor-quality ingredients palatable. Unfortunately, salty food desensitizes the tongue to salt.

A gradual reduction in salt exposure across the diet can be achieved without affecting consumers' taste perceptions; this strategy has been effective in several countries. Education, lobbying, and consumer demand would drive manufacturers to make more changes. A creative way to reduce salt intake and high-calorie, low-nutrient processed food might be a family assembly line that makes meals from good-quality ingredients and then freezes homemade TV dinners for those rushed days.

Quicksilver

Is there a difference in the amount of mercury in fish, whether you eat it raw or cook it? Is it possible to avoid the mercury in a fish by how you prepare it?

Mercury in fish is tightly bound to protein and is not removed during cooking processes such as smoking, broiling, baking, boiling, pan frying, and deep frying. Nor does the addition of lemon juice release mercury from its bound state. On the other hand, the cooking method affects the health benefits of fish, and the mercury concentration is strongly dependent on the type of fish.

Mercury originates from natural sources (volcanoes) and human sources (coal-fired power plants, waste incineration, gold mining). Organisms do not readily absorb mercury in the form in which it is usually released into the environment—metallic or inorganic mercury. Once rainwater carries inorganic mercury into lakes and oceans, microbes convert it into methylmercury, or organic mercury. (In chemistry, "organic" refers to carbon-containing compounds and has nothing to do with organic agriculture.)

Organic mercury is readily absorbed by organisms and accumulates in their tissues. It bioaccumulates in the aquatic food chain. In other words, short-lived species low in the food chain (such as shellfish and salmon) have low concentrations of mercury, while longer-lived predators (such as swordfish and shark) have high concentrations. The levels in albacore tuna are lower than those in swordfish but higher than those in salmon.

Industrial catastrophes that have resulted in mass consumption of high levels of mercury reveal that it is toxic to nerve cells, especially in children exposed during their early development. Studies of the effects of exposure to lower levels of mercury have been conflicting, but based on the possible risks, the U.S. Environmental Protection Agency and the U.S. Food and Drug Administration have issued advisories for women of childbearing age, pregnant women, nursing mothers, and young children.

At the same time, studies suggest that intake of fatty acids in fish by pregnant and nursing women is beneficial for the development of brain cells in infants. In addition, fish, except deep-fried fish, has well-documented cardiovascular benefits. For example, omega-3 polyunsaturated fatty acids in fish decrease the risk of heart attack by improving the fluidity of heart cell membranes.

In response to the confusion about the role of fish in a healthy diet, a 2006 article in the *Journal of the American Medical Association* concluded that, with the exception of a few fish species, the benefits of moderate fish consumption (two servings per week) outweigh the risks. The article recommends that nursing mothers and pregnant women avoid shark, swordfish, golden bass, and king mackerel; limit intake of albacore tuna to 6 ounces per week; and consult advisories for locally caught fish. But they should get at least 12 ounces per week of other fish and shellfish. See http://www.epa.gov/waterscience/fish/ for a list of mercury levels in different species and local fish advisories.

Index

C

I

J-K

L

M

N

O

P

Q-R

S

T

U

V

W-X

Y

Z